UN
OF Y
WITH PALMISTRY

The length of your fingers, shape of your palm, and pattern of your skin are more than just individual features . . . they're clues to who you are! Now you can use this "handy" guide to find out . . .

- The *real* meanings of the lines on your palms
- The truth about hand types—and their various combinations
- How to know yourself—and others—better through hand analysis
- The new discoveries that have revolutionized palmistry
- How our hands can reveal our character, our goals . . . and our destiny
- And much more!

BEYOND
PALMISTRY

BEYOND PALMISTRY:

THE ART AND SCIENCE OF MODERN HAND ANALYSIS

BEVERLY JAEGERS

Illustrated by Mary R.J. Cahn

BERKLEY BOOKS, NEW YORK

BEYOND PALMISTRY

A Berkley Book / published by arrangement with the author

PRINTING HISTORY
Berkley edition / November 1992

ISBN: 0-425-13403-2

A BERKLEY BOOK® TM 757,375
Berkley Books are published by The Berkley Publishing Group,
200 Madison Avenue, New York, New York 10016.
The name "BERKLEY" and the "B" logo
are trademarks belonging to Berkley Publishing Corporation.

PRINTED IN THE UNITED STATES OF AMERICA

10 9 8 7 6 5 4 3 2 1

To my husband, Ray, who always believed in me.

To Joan, to Carrie, to Charlene,
and to Kay McCauley—with love.

CONTENTS

PREFACE

Over twenty-seven years ago, I first discovered the mysteries of the human hand quite by accident. Dressed as a gypsy for a local Halloween party I was amazed when a man I didn't know placed his hand in mine and asked me to tell his future. I went along with the joke and told him he would shortly lose his wife. To my surprise, he snatched his hand back and stumbled away. Later I heard that he and his wife had separated only that morning. What had I seen? To this day I'm not sure.

In the months following that event, I searched libraries for books on the human hand and found many; but they were filled with conflicting information, folklore, and pseudo-fact. Little original research had been done in many years and what had been done seemed only to repeat earlier work. The field was filled with glaring deficiencies.

Disappointed yet still intrigued, I decided to do my own

research. I returned all the books and with an inky stamp pad and a pad of paper set out to print all the hands of my friends and relatives.

In a very short time, with a magnifying glass and often a headache, I was able to begin making some sense of hand patterns through comparison. My questions were persistent and often personal, but there was so much to know. What type of information is revealed on the hand? Personality? Health? The future? Did any traditional concepts of palmistry have validity?

In 1967 I was asked to teach a class in basic hand analysis in a local adult educational facility, which was an opportunity to broaden my search for facts.

My original class of ten included a clinical psychologist who shared many of his insights in human character, and a Roman Catholic nun who, as head of physical therapy at a local hospital, had access to handprints of persons already diagnosed with a multiplicity of diseases and physical conditions.

Other classes followed over the years, and through radio and television publicity, I was able to awaken much interest in the practical aspects of hand analysis. I was also able to handprint fascinating persons such as Lady Sarah Churchill, Pearl Bailey, and a host of gracious, generous, and charming entertainment and sports personalities. In 1973, on the CBS Regis Philbin Show, I found myself facing a person chosen from the audience and an avowed skeptic. Printing him on camera, I was quickly able to discern that he had a bent for the law, was a risk taker who loved action and brave deeds, and that he possessed a fine singing voice and might have sung in public.

Following a few other observations, I stopped and regarded him expectantly. He admitted, with a small smile, that he was a police officer, involved in study for a degree in criminal justice, was a motorcyclist, and as a youth had sung in a noted boys' choir.

The hand is like a tape recorder; it contains the coded information that renders each of us unique. Personality factors, inherited or developed during life, are present, as are markers illustrating most of the major and minor events of daily life. The hand can reveal past events, the recent past, and the present. It cannot foretell the future, but can indicate trends that will culminate in certain actions.

I have not found any personality factor nor physical, mental, or emotional problem that did not clearly show itself on the hand.

Probably the most crucial discovery of my research project was the existence of dermatoglyphics, or skin patterns. In traditional palmistry, the focus was on the major lines of the hand. Dermatoglyphics deals with fingerprints and the fingerprintlike patterns covering the entire palm. These patterns are so varied and so distinctively different from person to person that they can reveal most of the basic factors in every human personality kaleidoscope.

During the past three decades, I have continued to do empirical research and to teach hand analysis. And though much more is known today than when I first pored over old books in the library, there is still much to discover in the future.

I hope this book will reach an even larger audience and perhaps inspire others to begin their own odyssey into the intricacies of the human hand.

Whoever you are, what makes you *you* is on your hand. All you have been and all your untapped potential is there.

Welcome to the world of the hand.

—Beverly Jaegers

INTRODUCTION

You are about to enter a fascinating world, a world that will reveal much about yourself, your friends, and acquaintances.

Hands seem simply functional, not really having much to do with character, taste, and personality. Yet whether a person is a butterfly or a grouch, an Albert Einstein or an Edith Bunker, the hands, fingers, and nails can and do reveal one's every secret.

Most of us are aware that our fingerprints are unique. But most people don't know that all of us have unique skin patterns covering the entire surface of our palms.

Although you may have noticed that there are lines on the palm of your hand, do you realize that these lines can move, change, and even completely disappear from your hands?

If this is news to you, you are among the majority. Medical science tells us that the patterns on our hands develop during the fourth prenatal month—almost five months before birth. And according to a team of medical experts writing in *Medical World News*, it is now possible to predict congenital heart disease in the newborn, thus saving many lives that would have been lost. In addition, the researchers can predict susceptibility to some major disease groups— and may even show the ethnic background of any individual.

Palmistry is an old art, even inspiring the greeting card company, Hallmark, to put out a card showing how to tell fortunes by the hand's markings. Hand analysis, however, has shown that most of these methods cannot work, because the hand, like the person, is constantly changing to reflect what is happening to one. As a person moves into a new job or career, marries or divorces, has children or relocates to a new area, the hands will change to reflect these shifts as they occur in the course of life.

Even minor events like a cold, the flu, or undergoing a trauma or shock of any type will change and affect the hands temporarily, but not permanently.

In twenty-six years of looking at hands, I have seen no two alike. Each person's hands are a clear, individual mirror or map of his or her personality, physical condition and health, as well as all of the things that have happened throughout that lifetime.

Even more accurate than scientific psychological methods of vocational or aptitude testing, the fingerprints, the length, size, and shape of the thumb and fingers, the blocks that may appear across the finger sections, and even the intricate whorls, loops, and arches on the palms, can provide a perfect, individualized readout of the real skills, talents, and abilities the person possesses; as well as telling which career or job would be the best.

There is literally *no limit* to the things you can find out about yourself.

Let's begin to put the pieces together, and unveil the secrets that make you so uniquely *you*.

WHAT YOU WILL NEED TO BEGIN

You can use a photocopy for beginning analysis of your hand, which is quick and easy.

This will, however, only give you the outline, shape, and some of the major lines of the hand.

If you use a high-quality photocopying machine, and press lightly, you may be able to see some of the fingerprints and major pattern areas on the hand.

See How to Make Ink Prints for making one of several types of inked handprint. For complete accuracy and fine details of your life, your talents and aptitudes, and all the intricately fascinating things about you, it is best to have an inked print.

You will also need a magnifying glass, and a strong light. Some stores such as Walgreen's carry small magnifying glasses which have a tiny light built right into the handle.

Even a newborn baby's hand can be photocopied for analysis, as it is in some hospitals for identification purposes.

Keeping your prints in a folder makes them immediately accessible, but is not necessary. You may prefer an ordinary spiral-bound sketch pad.

Now we're ready. Take out your hand and let's go.

NOTE: You should always use your *dominant* hand to do analysis, whether from looking at it, photocopying it, or ink-printing it.

Your *dominant* hand is your right, for right-handed individuals.

If you are left-handed, print the left hand.

For the ambidextrous, print both hands. It will soon become evident which hand is dominant.

The dominant hand is slightly larger than the other, as is the dominant foot. You can use a ruler to measure.

Fascinating things can be found on both hands, but begin with your dominant hand and go on to the recessive.

1

YOUR HAND—
AND ITS SHAPE

Hand analysis is a system of self-knowledge that has no parallel in modern science. Although it's not a system of fortune-telling, it involves not only the lines and patterns of the skin's surface traditionally studied by fortune-tellers but also the shape, size, and curvature of the entire hand. Actually, hand shapes reveal the most interesting and easily recognizable facets of human personality. According to what type a person is—action, mental, technical, or emotional—you can forecast whether an individual will tend to be patient and easygoing or impatient and quick, whether a person is likely to grasp an idea rapidly, or require having things explained completely step-by-step and in detail.

The secret is revealed in the shape of their hands. A person who has a rounded hand may grasp concepts rapidly. The person with a thin, rectangular hand may want to think about all the factors in a situation before making a decision.

DOMINANT OR "PURE" TYPES

If you look closely at both of your hands, they may seem quite similar—or they may vary slightly in shape and size. It is normal for the hand you write with, your dominant hand, to be larger. For most of us, this is the right hand, which is considered to be your strongest hand. Right-dominant persons tend to have a larger right hand as well as a slightly larger right foot.

In working with this book, you will use your dominant hand, the one you eat, write, and unlock doors with.

Whether or not both hands are exactly alike in shape and size, you will find that the one you use most will have a shape that will either be a combination or fall directly into one of the following categories.

Action:	round palm, short fingers, few lines
Mental:	rectangular palm, long fingers, not many lines
Technical:	square palm, medium-long fingers, few lines
Emotional:	rectangular hand, long fingers, many lines

People whose hands look exactly like the illustrations are considered to be the "pure" types. Most hands will fall into one of these four categories, and can be easily typed by the shape of the palm and the length of the fingers. These shapes, sometimes known as dominant, signify predominant influences in your character. If you have a hand which doesn't seem to easily fit one of these categories—perhaps you have a thin rectangular palm with short fingers—you probably have a hand shape known as a blend. The discussion of blends is at the end of the chapter. The majority of the population falls into one of the four dominant or pure types following.

PURE TYPES

ACTION HANDS *(See Figure 1-A.)*

The Action hand is almost completely rounded, with a well-shaped curve at the outside edge of the palm, smooth skin, resilient texture, and well padded on the palm under fingers and thumbs with short fingers which are often widespread and have rounded tips.

The pure Action-type hand appears rounded in the palm, with fairly short, roundish fingers either the same length as the palm or slightly shorter. The fingertips are either softly rounded or almost pointed.

Action-type hands tend to have fewer lines than the other types. An Action-type hand with a great number of lines would tend to indicate the person is a worrier. This aspect is seen by a profusion of short and long lines beginning at the base of the thumb and shooting directly across the hand.

This type of hand belongs to quick-acting, energetic types who are usually on the go at all hours of the day or night.

Action hands with very slender, rounded fingers tend to be warm and sympathetic personalities, and they make friends quickly and easily. Action-handed individuals can be very entertaining companions and love conversation.

An Action hand with *very* short, thick fingers much shorter than the palm indicates a person who is blunt and forceful by nature, sometimes expressing startlingly frank opinions. They may be misunderstood by those who are

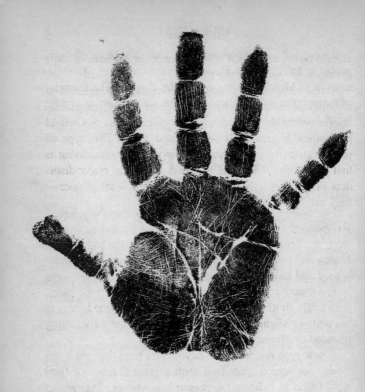

Action Hand

Rounded, curved palm;
widespread, shortish
rounded fingers; slim nails;
thumb and little finger at
wide angle. Warm, firm,
well-padded hand.

Figure 1-A

around them, and could cause resentment because of their penchant for speaking the truth.

Action hands signify people with quick intelligence who are often shrewd and aware individuals. They grasp ideas or concepts with ease, sailing through problems that would take others a great deal of time and study. This type of person seems to exude vitality, although the one caveat is that the Action's physical health is subject to many disorders. They generally will keep going until—all at once—they run out of energy.

Action-handed individuals often benefit from a nap or a period of rest sometime during the working day to refresh and increase their ability to sustain such intense activity.

This type of hand is usually good at getting what he wants. Persons in this group make fine parents, since they relish the excitement and challenge of life in general, and wish to pass on their own pleasure in achievement. They are bored with routine and tend to avoid dull, tedious jobs. Career indications include public service, journalism, personal representation, trial law, acting, Wall Street speculation, and anything that provides a challenge. They tend to hate housework of all types with a passion.

This is the hand type of Elizabeth Taylor, Johnny Carson, Charles Bronson, and *Pretty Woman*'s Julia Roberts.

KEY WORDS: ACTION, ENERGY, ACHIEVEMENT

MENTAL HANDS *(See Figure 1-B.)*

This type of hand is rectangular with long, smooth, unlined fingers. The palm and fingers are not necessarily the same length. The palm may be a bit longer than the fingers or the fingers may exceed the palm length by a half inch or so. From a distance, the Mental hand may be difficult to distinguish from the Emotional hand. The primary differ-

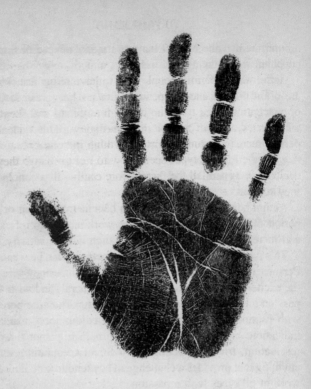

Mental Hand

Rectangular hand, long fingers with smooth or squared sides. Fingers may have round or squared-off tips. Moderate amount of lines. Warm, soft skin.

Figure 1-B

ence is that the Mental hand has many fewer lines on the palm. Also, the Mental hand has smooth, even-shaped fingers, while the Emotional tends to have larger knuckles.

The Mental-handed personalities are very varied. Characteristics range from the purely intellectual and skeptical, sardonic sort of person to the flighty-minded idealistic dreamer, including almost everything in between.

Some Mental types seem slow to react because they believe in having all the facts before coming to a conclusion. They tend to study problems from many sides.

Analytical and introspective, Mental types must fight against the tendency to fall victim to an ivory tower syndrome. They can lose touch with humanity, being so preoccupied with what is going on in their minds.

Ideals and concepts appeal to them and Mental types may often become true romantics because they feel life holds a secret that is waiting to be found if they can only keep looking long enough. Writing may be a professional or an emotional release for them.

Most pure Mental hands appear quiet, unassuming, and laid back. Not fans of display and pretense, they may have little patience with more bombastic types. They can, and do, lose patience with people who are stubborn, although, truthfully, they're frequently a bit bullheaded themselves.

As parents, they may be either extremely good, or dismally bad, depending on how easily they can put themselves on the child's level. They have patience, true concern, and an instinctive understanding of human motivations in general, though they may not be as perceptive about a *specific* person and his problems.

Mental-handed persons tend to feel life *should* be idyllic and in perfect order, and wonder why it is not. As they grow older, this utopian desire may lead to retreat from the hustle, bustle, and hurly-burly of the marketplace—and into a world of contemplation, research, and meditation. Many inventors have this hand.

A few Mental hands may retreat completely, sacrificing more self-oriented careers or lives to further or represent those of others. They are socially conscious and make fine social workers, jurists, business executives, and engineers or technicians. They have a flair for computers and anything that requires creative invention.

Since the Mental tends to be creative, a great many writers and journalists possess this long, rectangular hand. Thoughts, concepts, and ideals are their meat and drink. Since the Mental shape can become self-absorbed, when Mental types are blended with any of the other three types this usually adds more potential and motivation.

Psychologically, Mental types may feel no one quite understands them. Their tremendously creative imagination causes them to be introspective and self-conscious, even protective of their secret thoughts. This can lead to a sense of rejection or of being "different."

The Mental-hand person may seem to exist on caffeine and they are frequently heavy smokers.

One distinctive feature is that lines on this type of hand tend to change more often than on other shapes. Just as the mind is often active and busy with new plans, ideals, and projects, the hand may change to suit new outlooks. Life keeps changing focus. In fact, the Mental hand often has *so* many ideas and intentions that some are left on the drawing board because the Mental hand thinks things out so thoroughly he often decides *against* a project rather than continue it.

The late Michael Landon and Kirstie Alley have these hands, as do Jimmy Stewart and Betty White.

KEY WORDS: CREATIVE, THOUGHTFUL, ACTIVE, INTELLECTUAL

TECHNICAL HANDS *(See Figure 1-C.)*

This type of hand, once misrepresented by traditional palmists as elemental, unintelligent types, signifies intelligence and capacity. This hand, with its typical strongly squared-off large palm and long, thick but sensitive fingers usually connotes a capable personality. These large, clumsy-looking fingers are found on about 25 percent of the population. Technical hands may be found in the larger form on male subjects, as well as female. The female Technical hand is usually, however, much smaller, although the shape is exactly the same as the larger one.

Technical hands look powerful, and they are. But they may be found in research labs inventing artificial hearts, or even on the surgeon whose range of delicate, intricate hand movements look impossible for this large, often massive hand shape.

The men and women who possess this hand shape are usually dependable, resourceful, uncomplaining, and unassuming, yet brilliant in their own speciality.

Technical-handed individuals work at being efficient and feel that if a job is worth doing, it is worth doing well.

Honest, and possessing a well-balanced moral sense, the Technical hands can be trusted and depended upon. To some, they may seem a bit too methodical in their approach, yet this may be only the outward manifestation of a fine mind which is hard at work on some ultimately successful plan that takes time and thought to achieve. This type can and does take on intensely challenging jobs that require concentration over long periods of time. If forced to take dynamic, fast-reaction types of employment, they will compensate by acquiring a hobby that requires intricate craftsmanship. This is the man or woman who may be running

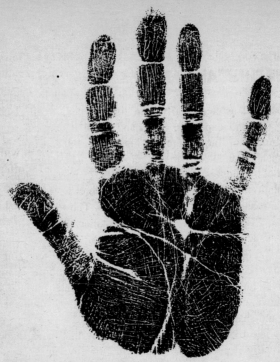

Technical Hand

Square palm, strong, rounded or squared-off fingers. Wide nails, fingers closer together. Low-set thumb, which may have an angular base. Warm, hard, flattish palm, thick smooth skin.

Figure 1-C

a large corporate setup, yet spends most of his or her leisure hours in activities such as woodworking, carving, painting, collecting and repairing antiques, and similar pursuits. These activities are their own personal and very specialized way of gaining time for relaxation and refreshment.

The Technical-hand type has only two drawbacks. The owner may be prone to nervous tension when faced with a difficult or constricting situation, and unless relief is offered may sometimes become prey to real or imagined illnesses. Another possibility is that if the individual is boxed in by circumstances he cannot control, the Technical-handed may fear he is being persecuted.

The majority of Technical-handed, however, skillfully avoid situations which are unmanageable or uncontrollable. If unimpeded, they are consistently successful in achievement as well as charming in their outer charismatic warmth and generosity.

Both Clint Eastwood and Carroll O'Conner have this kind of hand, as does Sylvester Stallone. On the female side are Barbara Bush and the late American aviatrix Amelia Earhart.

KEY WORDS: SUCCESSFUL, BROAD-MINDED, TRUSTWORTHY

EMOTIONAL HANDS *(See Figure 1-D.)*

Emotional hands are the most complex of the pure types. Although they tend to react more slowly than Action types, their emotions are often deeper and more lasting in nature.

In appearance, the Emotional hand is often long and thin, with delicate skin, and very pale in color. The hand has dozens of random-appearing lines crossing the palm. In appearance, these lines look like those on a map, or on a hand soaked in water, with large and small ones running in all directions.

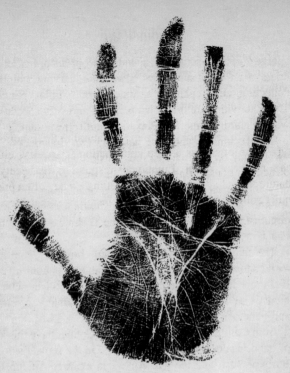

Emotional Hand

Long hand, slim to thin, rectangular shape, with prominent knuckles and thin thumb. Many lines make skin look wrinkled. Skin usually soft, cool, and dry. May have loose skin between fingers.

Figure 1-D

The fingers of the Emotional type are also long and slender, frequently wrinkled-looking along their length, and with strongly enlarged knuckles. The hand may look as if it belongs to an older person, even when the owner is a teenager.

A love of romance and drama is natural to the Emotional type, who often has a deep appreciation for poetry, either as a reader or writer. Emotionals respond to the beauty of nature, and are drawn to outdoor settings. They often prefer quiet solitude to the pressure and bustle of social life, yet they can excel in social situations. Creative party-givers, they tend to be attracted to strong, interesting types of men or women and seem to absorb energy from being around persons with determination and drive.

In family situations, they may find parenthood a challenge, yet can be the best of loving caregivers. They are quite capable of sacrificing themselves for an ideal or for someone they love, whether a child, a spouse, an elderly relative, or friend.

They may never receive a word of thanks for such service, but seem outwardly content since they do not require constant reassurance. More females than males tend to be Emotional.

It is difficult for the Emotional-handed to forget the past and pursue new ventures. They are nostalgic and revere the time-honored, while rejecting the new and bold. They are repelled by bizarre or frightening things, and possess a vivid fantasy life. An interesting hand, unusual to find in the pure type.

Both Katharine Hepburn and Jeanne Dixon have this hand.

KEY WORDS: SENSITIVE, CREATIVE

BLENDED HANDS

Some hands do not quite fit into either the pure or dominant types. Your palm may be round, but your fingers long and knuckly. Your fingers may be short, but there may be a great many small lines covering the hand.

If this is the case, you will probably fall into one of the blended types.

Example: round palm, long fingers, many lines.

This hand would fall into the Action category, but the long fingers and lines would add the effects of the Sensitive hand. Your type—Action/Sensitive.

Example: rectangular palm, few lines, short tapering fingers.

Blended hands and their distinguishing characteristics are given in this section. Most blended hands bestow upon their owner just a bit of something "extra" and may add spice to the brew.

HOW TO DETERMINE

Normally, the shape of the palm itself will determine the dominant part of the blend. If the palm is round, look in the Action category. If the palm is square, look under Technical; and if the palm is rectangular you will look under Mental, if there are few lines, or under Emotional if there are many lines showing on the palm.

It is easy to see palm shapes, even in a baby or child, so you will have little difficulty in finding the right blend to match the hand.

ACTION BLENDS

ACTION/MENTAL *(See Figure 1-E.)*

This is a very desirable type of blend, as the force of the Action hand is enhanced and softened by the intellectual nature of the Mental type.

This hand features an extremely rounded palm, with long, tapering fingers. This is the hand often painted in Renaissance portraits of the Madonna.

The Action/Mental combination results in a more mature and slower type of activity and judgment than pure Action types, with a greater potential for activity than is common to the pure Mental type. Individuals with this hand put ideas to work.

ACTION/EMOTIONAL

This hand is quite round in the palm, but with much longer knobby-knuckled fingers and a great many very fine lines covering the palm and giving the appearance of being soaked in water overnight.

This can be a troubled hand. Often the activity of the Action is overpowered by Emotional sensitivity. This type is rare.

ACTION/TECHNICAL

Action-type rounded hands are squared off by a blunting of the curved shape, almost ending up as a bulgy square. The fingers of the blended type are thick and stubby, or thick and clumsy-looking.

This type is a "doer" and an "achiever," with slightly slower thought processes. Action/Technicals make good

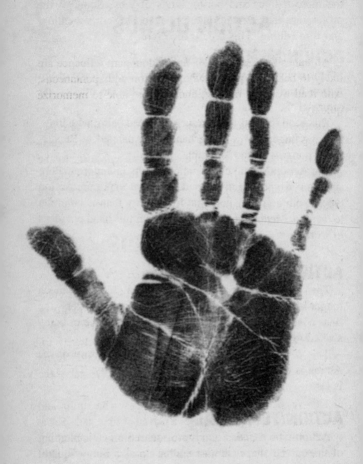

Figure 1-E: Action/Mental

workers as they have the patience and the application for the more tedious and boring kinds of jobs. Some of the professions they do well in are bookkeeping, dressmaking, and film editing. This type is also rare.

All hands that have Action as the dominant influence are likely to belong to people who are warm and spontaneous; who read well and rapidly, and who are able to memorize quickly.

Another trait typical of both Action blends and pure Action types is what might be called "elevator" moods, as they can range from the highest level of euphoria to the depths of despair in a short period of time. However, although this mood shift may seem erratic, Action types are seldom drug or alcohol abusers.

MENTAL BLENDS

MENTAL/ACTION *(See Figure 1-F.)*

A common blend, this hand has a long, clean, rectangular palm, with fingers either the exact length of the palm, or shorter than the palm. An easy way to spot this type is that while Mental hands usually hold their fingers closely together or just slightly separated, the Mental/Action blend will show the wide separation of fingers more typical of the Action hand.

This is the hand of a creative "doer" who mulls and designs his or her plans out over a period of time and then—watch out. Mental/Action types use continuous mental activity and determination to reach their goals. They will fight for their dreams with great tenacity.

MENTAL/EMOTIONAL

This blend is uncommon and often difficult to distinguish from the pure Emotional type. The almost perfectly rectan-

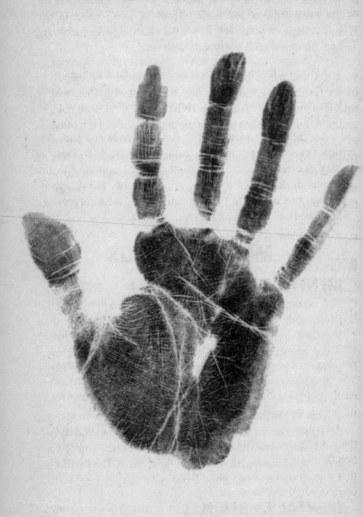

Figure 1-F: Mental/Action

gular hand may be found with long, rounded fingers and almost squared-off fingertips; but the palmar area is covered with a myriad of fine lines belonging to Emotional hands. The knuckles may be slightly enlarged.

Mental/Emotional hands often belong to frustrated people with tremendous ideals and goals, who yet may be unsure of the result, or they may hesitate to take the gamble, and thus lose the chance to achieve. When they do take the risk, and something happens to upset the applecart, this type often gives up in despair and retreats completely into noncompetition. Many great stars of stage and screen have had this type of hand. They are more comfortable pretending to be someone else on the stage of life, rather than the person they actually are.

The Mental/Emotional blend appears in less than 5 percent of hands.

MENTAL/TECHNICAL

This hand is long and square-looking with a rectangular palm, powerful thumb, and more lines than the pure Mental type. The fingers are very long and smooth and usually softly rounded at the tips or blunted. Nails are flat or slightly arched and broad, with large moons. There are few skin patterns on the palm, but those that appear are quite large. This fine, workable blend where both traits complement each other has a firm texture and is easily recognized for its length and power.

It may, if it belongs to a man, be so large it will cover the entire page and run off the top or bottom edge. Arnold Schwarzenegger has this hand, which is often deceptive in that it seems to connote brute strength, yet has hidden depths of intellect and determination.

Mental/Technical types are smart and aggressive. They have good ideas and will pursue them to their conclusion.

Hands of this sort are found running large international corporations, following some lucrative path of entrepreneurship, or are busily working their way up to the top in their chosen professions.

The Mental group of hands are fascinating and attractive, yet they must remember to keep their feet on the ground while they are reaching for the stars.

TECHNICAL BLENDS

TECHNICAL/ACTION

The square or rectangular palm, shortish fingers, high padding, and strong thumb make this a distinctive, capable-looking hand. This is a good blend, since the deep restlessness and desire of Action may, if the hand has very short and widespread fingers, overcome the tendency to slower progress of the Technical hand. The thumb may be low-set and seem to be too close to the index finger. However, if the thumb is as spread as the rest of the fingers, the blend is much more workable and less sensitive to stress.

These individuals can excel in their chosen career, and are capable of operating under almost unbearable stress and tension. Correspondingly, they may be prone to ulcers, migraine headaches, allergies, and other stress-related conditions.

TECHNICAL/MENTAL *(See Figure 1-G.)*

One of the finest of the subtypes, this square-palmed, long-fingered hand is an earth mover when it is stirred to work toward a goal. The deep insight and creative intellect of the Mental hand is added to the thorough thought proc-

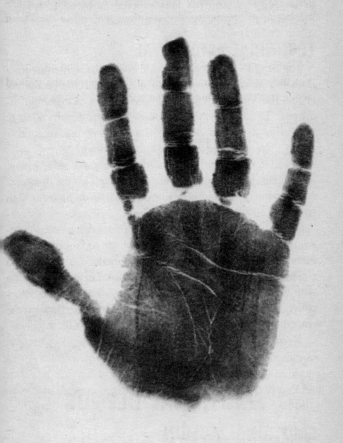

Figure 1-G: Technical/Mental

esses of Technical types, thus enriching the personality and its capacity to achieve. This subtype or blend forms 80 percent of the Technical group of hands.

TECHNICAL/EMOTIONAL

The hand is easily recognizable due to the numerous fine lines that cover the usually clean, clear palm of the Technical hand. The knuckles may be knobbier than is common to the pure Technical type. This complicates matters by adding indecision to the usual capable authority of the Technical shape, thus causing slower reaction to stimuli.

Because of the influence of the Emotional side, many good ideas, goals and projects might be left on the drawing board. This type hand needs to concentrate on building the confidence to go forward with plans.

Subject to self-doubt and fear at times, these are people who are prone to gastrointestinal problems and reproductive-system disorders if female, urinary if male.

This hand type excels in careers involved in helping others with their problems, for they have deep sympathy and empathy. They are also good singers, writers, and sculptors since music, shape, color, and form appeal to them.

EMOTIONAL BLENDS

EMOTIONAL/ACTION

In this blend, the rounded palm and widespread fingers of Action are overlaid with the multitude of lines belonging to Emotional, and would indicate a person who suffers from tightly compressed and controlled aspects of emotion, liable to explosions and nervous stress. If this type has learned self-control, the individual is capable of doing an enormous volume of work or accomplishing overwhelming and difficult tasks with ease.

Persons with this type hand would be found crying in sentimental movies, and would read historical novels and biographies in prefence to vivid adventure, science-fiction or fantasy.

EMOTIONAL/MENTAL *(See Figure 1-H.)*

Recognized by smoother fingers and knuckles above the many-lined palm, this is a tremendously effective combination. Here is a personality type who would be found running a large charity or joining in political-action groups. When they believe in a cause, they become mighty advocates.

In this hand, the intellect of the Mental type supports and adds to the emotional content of the typical Emotional hand. One of the best blends, career choices might include overseas travel, anything to do with cruises or travel publicity, romance writing, fantasy writing, or moviemaking.

EMOTIONAL/TECHNICAL *(See Figure 1-I.)*

A very unusual blend, it is identified by a smoother finger joint, and fewer lines than the typical Emotional hand.

The Technical qualities water down the Emotional qualities, and add a measure of practicality to the personality. It is a blend which creates a very unusual sort of person, as they find it difficult to choose a direction and stick to it. Indecisive, they may confuse others with their lightninglike mood swings. As to careers, they make fine actors and columnists and enjoy any job that involves animals.

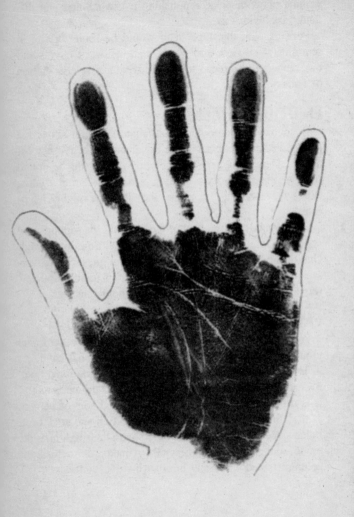

Figure 1-H: Emotional/Mental

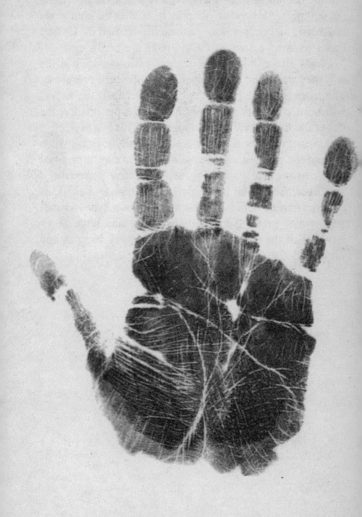

Figure 1-I: Emotional/Technical

For the beginning hand analyzer, it is wise to draw around the outline of the hand as you print it, or after the photocopy has been made. This way characteristics such as knobby knuckles or an extremely curved palm are easily seen.

Hands also exhibit some of their basic attitudes in the way they are placed on the paper, or the photocopy machine. The more open the personality, the wider apart the fingers will be. Conversely, the more held in the personality, the closer the fingers will be held together. This is a protective trait, and if a person's fingers are held tightly together when making the print, it may be wise not to ask very personal questions, as this is a retiring, self-protective personality.

Caveat: Be careful when assigning a type to a child, as children may be born with what looks like one type of hand, and as they grow, the hand will change and settle down into one of the pure types as the personality matures and firms up.

2

FINGERNAILS AND WHAT THEY REVEAL ABOUT YOU

Since the shape and size of your fingers can reveal dozens of secrets about inner personality, it is not surprising that the fingernails, too, show a great deal about a person's psychological profile and even their health. Nails can even tell a chiropractor *exactly* what is wrong with the neck and spine if there has been an injury in these areas.

Just as with shapes of hands, there are different types of nails. One hand may even display a few types of nails, although most hands will possess only one type of nail. On a hand of the Action variety, it would be common to find the nails of the Psychic or Sensitive type. A Mental hand might have Sensitive or Frank nails. A Technical hand would be likely to have Frank or Mental nails. The Emotional hand often has Sensitive nails, and a combination of one or more types is likely.

NAIL TYPES

There are at least seven distinct types of fingernails: Psychic, Sensitive, Frank, Able, Hand Worker, Critical, and Wedge. *(See Figure 2-A.)* A hand may have one type of nail or a mixture. An analyst cannot do a full and accurate analysis of any hand without taking the nails into account.

Traditionally palmists gave meanings to the nail, but these associations were often faulty. For example, the nail used to be associated with psychological types, while now it is associated with personal aptitudes, creativity potential and even vocational aptitudes in many cases.

When taking a print or photocopy of the hand, the nails should be observed closely, and a note made at the tip of the fingerprint, giving the type of nail. Check each nail individually, in case of varying types.

THE PSYCHIC NAIL (Mental)

Although this word may suggest an exotic nail type, this type is quite common, found on a great many hands, and not relegated to the hands of psychics.

This nail is narrow, often fairly long in the nail bed (which is the pinkish section of the nail) with a high curved arch, and a rounded or slightly almond-shaped base, never a squared-off cuticle base.

Women with this nail frequently use nail polish, because their nails are beautifully enhanced with some added color. They are usually very pink nails with very white moons at the bottom and white tips with a high curvature.

Traditionally, these types have a tendency to lung prob-

Seven Basic Types of Fingernail

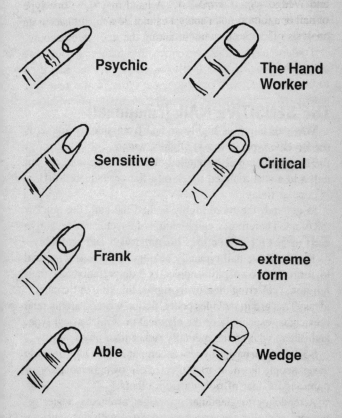

Psychic

The Hand Worker

Sensitive

Critical

Frank

extreme form

Able

Wedge

Figure 2-A

lems. Common colds often settle deeply into the chest and may cause a heavy cough that hangs on. They are also susceptible to airborne allergies caused by such things as insect spray in home or garden, diesel exhaust, and even hair sprays, if used in excess.

If this nail is found on three or more fingers of either hand, the owner is almost certainly endowed with highly sensitive intuition and seems to just "know" things about people as if without sensory clues.

THE SENSITIVE NAIL (Emotional)

This nail is not as highly arched from side to side as is the Psychic type, and it is slightly wider.

These nails are also rounded off at the base, and are cut either in a soft rounded shape or a flat cut (squared-off) as is popular today.

In general, the more highly arched the nail, the quicker the mind. Therefore, a combination of Psychic and Sensitive nails means the person uses his mind well and profitably.

The Sensitive nail typically belongs to persons who tend to form their own philosophies or interpretations of their religion, preferring their own original thinking to "canned" ideas. This group includes poets, fiction writers, artists, and musicians, especially of the classical or semiclassical type, and others who create mentally rather than physically.

Sometimes a basic shyness accompanies this nail, making these people hesitant to project their own personality or opinions for fear of ridicule from others.

A tendency to glandular or weight problems, water retention, and allergies may be associated with the Sensitive nail.

THE FRANK NAIL (Dependable)

This nail is a little wider than the first two types and is flatter over the entire surface. It can be evenly rounded in shape, or may look almost squared-off at the sides. The cuticle base may also be almost straight across, or very slightly rounded, and the tip is usually only slightly curved. The cuticle usually grows fast, and covers the base completely.

This type tends to have a balanced personality—people who are secure in themselves. Frank types are great party guests, enjoy good conversation, and usually love to talk to interesting people and to listen to music.

Often a very active mind and body go with this nail. Sympathetic and outgoing by nature, this type has a basic friendliness and is often receptive toward others.

If the hand also has a long tip section, the longest section of the little finger, the owner may speak his or her mind without forethought, and often causes tense moments. If you want a true opinion, ask someone with this type of nail.

This is a fairly common nail, found on a great number of hands.

Some people with the Frank nail have a tendency toward malfunctions of major organs.

THE ABLE NAIL (Creative)

A squarish nail, often almost flat at both ends, it is common on both male and female hands. It belongs to very capable people who do any job well.

The finger itself is often smooth, but more often knotted slightly at the middle joint (indication of practicality).

This nail is usually found on Technical hands.

The color of the hand and nail is usually a light pink. If insufficient oxygen is being utilized, it will be pale or slightly tinged with yellow.

Typical careers include craftsman, creative housekeeper, career mother, nurse, musician, computer operator and programmer, secretary, lawyer, and politician.

It can appear on some hands only on the thumb, while the fingers may be of a Psychic, Sensitive, or Frank shape. If this is true, it indicates one whose job or career is not the only purpose in life, and the owner may be found pursuing many hobbies. This type often works well with children, handicapped persons, or those who are ill or in need of help—a really nurturing type.

A predisposition to problems with the gastrointestinal system or the circulatory system may be present when all nails on a hand are of this type.

THE HAND WORKER NAIL (Multitalented)

In traditional palmistry, this broad, flat nail was thought to belong to people of inferior intelligence; however, many surgeons, engineers, dentists, draftsmen, and architects who use their fingers for delicate, fine movements have these nails. So much for traditional palmistry.

This nail is distinctive in appearance as it is square or slightly rounded and flat. The base is wide and almost perfectly straight across. The cuticle does not grow up the fingernail and is usually somewhat hard in texture.

On males this nail is quite wide, though not quite so wide in females. The fingers on which these nails are found are very powerful-looking. These fingers may appear to be squared-off as well, rather than rounded. The knuckles are usually more wrinkled and the skin looks looser than on most hands.

The fingers may appear stiff, but are actually extremely

flexible, often exceptionally so. This nail is often found on the Technical-shaped hand, and signifies good mechanical ability.

Hand worker types often love good music, are excellent dancers, possess a fine sense of rhythm, and may love sports as a physical outlet or stress-reliever. If their career is in sports of any variety they usually excel.

These nails also indicate fine mechanical ability, and add a creative dimension to any hand.

Not lovers of show, they may seem to be shy or laid back in their appearance. But there are surprising depths in this overall personality. It takes them time to trust, but when they do, they do so completely. Trustworthy and honest themselves, they expect the same in others.

Because they are so good at presenting a calm exterior, and holding things inside, they are often subject to stress-related arterial problems, varicose veins, diseases of the arteries, and sometimes congestive or irritative problems of the genitourinary and reproductive systems.

THE CRITICAL NAIL (Precision)

A noticeably short nail with considerable flesh showing on both sides, this nail poses a problem for women since it is difficult to manicure and often does not grow to the end of the finger.

These nails may also be set very low on the finger, or so high that the nail looks abnormally short. Often this person's toenails are short as well.

In extreme cases, this nail may be much wider than it is long.

The Critical nail is often found on the hands of persons who are very vocal and must make some type of small noise almost continuously. If they have no one to talk with, they will turn on the radio or even the television in another room, just for the sound. They abhor silence and are restless when alone.

Owners of Critical nails are often, though not necessarily, critical of others, ready and willing to speak their minds.

These types sometimes lack tact and sensitivity, and can be considered a bit pushy, aggressive, touchy, or proud. They may not handle failure well and can become stymied or self-conscious. If one or more of the fingers is strongly curved toward the index finger or the little finger, this reveals a keen desire for a fulfilling life.

Critical nails indicate a high degree of nervousness, either displayed openly or held in. They may be liable to problems of the nervous system. Some may compensate with indulgence in alcohol or drugs of the recreational type.

Many of the problems are psychosomatic in origin.

If only one Critical nail appears on a hand, the person will not display the entire spectrum of characteristics given above. If several of the nails are of the Critical type, care should be taken in dealing with these individuals, thus helping to counter some of their excessive temperament factors.

THE WEDGE NAIL (Irritable)

This is an unusual nail, almost triangular in shape, narrowest at the bottom and widest at the fingertip. The cuticle breaks the narrowing effect, or the nail might appear almost to end in a point.

Wedge-shaped nail types can be subject to violent extremes of mood. If the person has a hand that is also wedge-shaped, and that exhibits an overdeveloped thumb with a double-looped fingerprint, this may indicate a person who is inclined to solve his or her problems in a physical way. This is not necessarily bad, as often this type relieves stress in violently active games such as handball, soccer, hockey, rugby, tennis, aerobics, or football.

Sometimes this nail represents lack of some vitamin or nutrient during the prenatal months.

It is found on the hands of gentle, reflective people as well as those of the more physical type. In this case, it may represent a hereditary factor involving some more vigorous ancestral strain which has been sublimated or overcome in the present generation.

One weakness is that psychological illnesses may occur.

I have never seen a case where all five nails on one hand were wedge-shaped. One or two wedge nails may signify fondness for physical activity.

NAIL CONDITIONS

THIN NAILS

This condition is usually caused by nutritional factors. Thin nails break easily and are translucent. The nail usually is deep pink, with a large moon and very white tip. Circulatory problems may go with this nail, and if yours are thin nails, you should be careful to keep your body active and healthy, with plenty of fresh air and exercise, adding vitamins and fresh, raw foods to the diet.

Nails which are just a light pink do not fall into this category.

A yellowish tint to the nail may indicate either a slight jaundice, or too much beta-carotene. If you are taking this supplement, or adding a great amount of carrots or other yellow vegetables to your diet, stopping or cutting down will return the nails to the normal color.

According to folklore white spots on the nails predict a new baby, a wedding, or a death in the family. Not true. The real reason may be that you are lacking in calcium, magnesium, and probably the B-complex vitamins.

Nails with dark coloration in the lower end, sometimes seen as a dark red over the entire nail or a crimson edge above the white moon, indicate respiratory or circulatory problems, and you should advise the individual to get a physical checkup.

THICK NAILS

A rather thick nail may indicate a depletion in the body of Vitamin A. It can also be a sign of a stress-related irritation that may be of long standing and is being held in. Persons with quick, hot tempers usually have thin nails, while persons who are slow to anger (but hold grudges) have thicker nails.

LOOSE NAILS

It may sound unusual, but if you have one or more nails which tend to loosen from the fingers on your dominant hand only, it could be caused by squeezing lemons, limes, or oranges by hand. Many bartenders, cooks, and other people who juice citrus fruits have this problem. If it affects one or more of your nails and you do squeeze citrus, simply wash your hands thoroughly, and use a cuticle stick to clean under the nails. If you've had it for some time, put a small amount of rubbing alcohol in a glass and soak the fingertips for ten minutes. This will relieve the condition.

CROOKED NAILS

Amazingly enough, problems with the neck and spine cause the nails to bend and curve. It is possible to easily diagnose a back problem by a simple examination of the fingernails. We will cover this further in Chapter 7, Your Hand and Your Health.

FLUTED NAILS

Light fluting or visible lines running from top to bottom of your nails may indicate thyroid problems. When this is present the thyroid should be checked.

See Chapter 7 for other indications of thyroid problems.

TRAUMA TRENCHES

If a fingernail shows a fairly deep side-to-side indentation, it is an indication of a shock or trauma. It can be caused by illness, loss of job or a loved one, or an accident. Any deep shock can leave such an indentation. Since nails grow from beneath the cuticle and slowly grow toward the tip of the finger, it is possible to date the trauma by where it appears on the nail. Fingernails take six months to grow out completely. If the shallow trench appears near the cuticle, the event occurred recently. Halfway up it would be three months previously. Near the end of the nail, it would be six months previously. As it takes almost nine months for the thumbnail to grow out all the way, it is possible to date traumatic events or illness more accurately.

NAIL BITING AND BREAKAGE

In some cases, it is possible to discover what types of stresses bother a chronic nail-biter by checking which fingernails are bitten.

A. THUMB: Personal will is being blocked or person is being forced to do something.

B. INDEX: Possible lack of self-esteem or self-confidence; person may be having problems at work.

Key to Bitten Fingernails

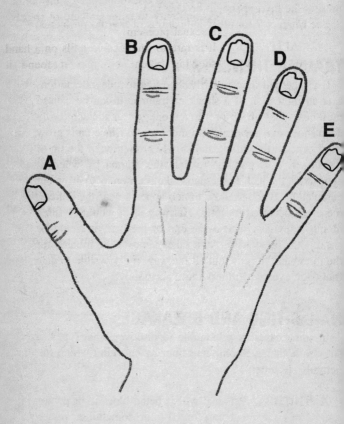

Figure 2-B

C. MIDDLE:	Usually a sign of a feeling of guilt or an emotional problem that cannot be easily solved.
D. RING:	Fear of failure often causes people to bite this nail, as does loneliness, self-doubt.
E. LITTLE:	An inability to communicate or (rarely) a sexual problem.
ALL:	It is rare to find all five nails on a hand showing bitten ends but if found it indicates a general life problem of major proportions. Nervous apprehension may also cause an individual to gnaw on all of his nails.

Stress in one of these areas of life often results in the nail actually breaking off at the tip, or becoming brittle and breaking often. Once the problem in that area of life is cleared up, the nail will return to its normal strength and growth.

Nails take about six months to grow from cuticle bed to tip, although the thumb may take from nine months to a year.

3

LOOPS, SWOOPS, AND SWIRLS ON THE HAND

All of us are familiar with fingerprints, but although you may never have noticed them, there are some interesting, unique skin patterns not only on the tips of the fingers, but on the fingers themselves, and everywhere across the palm. These loopings and tiny skin patterns appear only on the palm area of the hand and on the bottoms of the feet.

Fingerprints were known to law enforcement agencies for decades before someone finally figured out that everyone's hand was composed of completely different prints and that these markings were absolutely individual.

The largest number of fingerprints on file are in the records of the FBI, Scotland Yard in England, and Interpol, the International Police agency. Hundreds of thousands of criminals can be identified by their fingerprints and the very specialized patterns on their palms.

Although these fingerprints are collected daily by these large information-gathering agencies, skin patterns also contain *meaning*. These prints can indicate a practical or fanciful personality. They reveal whether a person has a sense of humor; a good memory; personal attraction and charisma; and how fast or how slowly you think and react.

DERMATOGLYPHICS

The scientific term for these swirling patterns on the skin is dermatoglyphics. The word means "skin-carving," an awkward way to refer to skin patterns which form on fourth-month-old fetuses.

The average human hand will have a pattern on each fingertip, and two loops somewhere on the palm. The patterns on fingertips may or may not be loops. The classifications are easy to determine and to interpret, once the print is taken. A fast fingerprint set may be made with an ordinary office stamp pad, which gives a clear and readable print. It is best, however, to use a speedball ink, which is available at hobby and art stores. (See How to Make Ink Prints.)

These patterns fall generally into one of the following types.

ARCH

There are two types of arch: one is a flat arch and the other is a highly tented arch. There is no looping of the print on the finger.

This print is a sign of high intelligence, and a mind that is always asking questions. The individual with this print formation is usually both simple and direct (Frank). If you ask his or her opinion, be prepared to hear the truth.

Arches are found on the fingers of persons who are reliable and honest, unless the remainder of the hand is weak.

It is a somewhat conservative formation, and may be

Tented arch

found on the hands of a person who either appreciates or collects things from the past.

Moral values are quite strong, especially in maturity. It is possible that the person may have a "past," due to mistakes made before the personality matured, as this print also indicates a sensuality of nature and a longing for sexual fulfillment.

On the Mental or Action hand, this print is a reinforcing force. On the Emotional or Technical hand, it would be supportive and would enrich the intellect, as well as adding stability to the personality. Arches represent a steady, capable, can-do factor in the psychological makeup.

In a weak hand with twisted fingers, it will create a strong conflict, as the person is unable to control his or her direction in life and may feel guilty about it because he or she feels the failure deeply.

In general, it is a strong, helpful print found on the hands of many geniuses and deep thinkers. It is especially good when found on the index finger only, or the index and middle fingers only. When it appears, add depth of intellect to your analysis of the hand!

Note: the higher the arch tents up in the middle, the stronger the intelligence may be.

KEY WORDS: INTELLIGENCE, CREATIVITY

LOOP

This print is distinctive, with the pattern seeming to enter from the little finger side of the hand, looping around and then leaving again from whence it came. It is an indication of a fast-moving mind, which may be keen and sharp if the hand is strong, or it could represent a bit of shallowness on a weak hand with crooked fingers and a deep hollowed palm.

Owners of this type print can take the best of the ideas and assets of others and make them distinctively their own. As perceptive individuals, they are able to see the talents or imperfections of others better than they can their own, and may often lose sight of their own faults and virtues in their interest in those with whom they associate or interact on a consistent basis.

Helpful and interested, loop-fingered people make good listeners, good friends and companions, as well as good advisors. People are drawn to them because they *will* listen. They are usually most interested in teaching or advising those whose talents and interests lie in the same directions

Loop

as their own. Very competent and skillful persons, they can sometimes scatter their energies because of wide-ranging interests (too many irons in the fire). People with loop-fingered hands may be impatient with others who seem to think slowly or cannot grasp concepts easily. Able to follow instructions easily, understand quickly, these individuals are usually always reaching out for better perception and understanding.

All types of hands are supported by this print pattern. If looking for a loophole in a situation, even in a very complex or legal quandary, ask the person who has three or more looped fingerprints. They think quickly and can find escape hatches when needed.

They are open-minded people, enjoy looking into new subjects, possess great curiosity, and often are interested in the unusual or baffling. Attention span, however, can be fairly short.

Loops most often are found on Action, Mental, and Technical hands, slightly less often on Emotional hands. Loops indicate a "normal" person—insofar as there is such a thing. They signify a person who is involved in life and has a spirit of adventure.

KEY WORDS: FLEXIBILITY, CURIOSITY, INVOLVEMENT

WHORLS OR BULL'S-EYES

This very special pattern loops around in a circle or an oval. It may look like an eye, sometimes complete with pupil and iris. It functions almost exactly as does an eye, only in a mental sense rather than a physical one.

Wherever it appears, it is a sign of a very outstanding, nonconformist personality. With a whorl on *every* finger, the man or woman would be an extremely remarkable personality, following no rules except his or her own, perhaps possessing one or more types of genius.

Plain whorl

Index Finger. This whorl is known as the *gift of perception*, signifying one who can see truth. Its possessors cannot be lied to and are very hard to fool. They have a difficult childhood, as a rule, for they see those around them only too clearly and are disappointed or disillusioned by what they see. It is more comfortable to accept the facades people present, and the owners of the bull's-eye index see beyond that into the truth behind the false surface. Many great painters and architects have had this print.

Middle Finger. This placement signifies one who has a *gift of organization*. If involved with electronics or computers they are capable of astonishing feats. They almost instantly place disparate items into categories and can see relationships that would escape anyone else. This placement is much easier to live with than the index finger position. Just stand back and let them have free rein.

Ring Finger. A whorl on this fingertip indicates a person with the *gift of discrimination*, one who can spot a defect or a flaw in any material object, concept, plan, or undertaking. If some factor hasn't been taken into account, this individual can spot it, and tell you what is wrong at a glance. One with this print may be a perfectionist, bothered by a picture hanging slightly off center on the wall, and if building a house or decorating an apartment, should remember always to do it on his own, because he'll never be happy with anyone else's ideas. If one doesn't have the print, but is planning to open a new business, to market an invention, or begin some new venture, he should find a person with the bull's-eye whorl on the ring finger to look it over before he begins.

A good many lawyers and inventors have this placement.

Little Finger. A *gift of communication*! This person may write, sing, do public speaking. He or she may be politically minded, or may write the speeches for other candidates.

Music company executives may also have the bull's-eye on the little finger, as might publishers, editors, agents, and anyone whose field is communication.

If their career has not taken this direction, or the print is found on the hand of a child, the individual should be advised to direct his or her education into some form of mass media. Endearingly, the person with the whorl on the little finger can and does talk your right ear off and then begins on the left. Batten the hatches and *listen*.

Thumb. A very powerful place to have a whorled fingerprint, revealing the *gift of willpower and forcefulness*. This person may be a genius, a philanthropist, an executive—or a master criminal! He or she has an exceptionally determined will, knows what he wants, and goes for it! The whorled thumb hates to live by anyone else's rules (which is true to some degree of anyone with bull's-eye fingerprints), but the bull's-eye thumb will make his own rules, always.

Key to Whorl or Bull's-eye Fingerprints

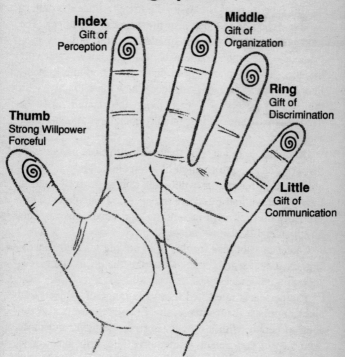

The possibility of a whorl appearing on any finger is one of the strongest reasons for taking an inked print of a hand. The photocopy usually will not show it, and if one is there, it may influence the entire hand analysis.

LOOP/ARCH

This type of print is classified by itself, since the pattern is both arched *and* looped near the center of the finger. The loop portion is often much smaller than the ordinary loop print, and the arched pattern is clearly in view, overlying the top. The loop/arch print indicates open-mindedness. People with this type of print accept new ideas readily, with the mental reservation that more information will be needed—and they will eventually make certain that they find it.

Often able to retain what they read with ease, people with this print absorb information like a sponge. They are probably good at figuring as well, even doing involved math in their heads without reference to paper or a calculator. They probably do their own income tax and handle investments and financial decisions independently.

Career possibilities for this print are often found in writing, creative research in science and medicine, or other areas involving new ideas.

The person is interested in a wide range of subjects and likes to pursue them intensively. Loop/arch prints also belong to people with a turn for abstract thought, and those who have a very retentive memory. This print belongs to readers, thinkers, and philosophers, as well as good judges of character.

On Technical hands, the print adds a searching intellect and a spark of brilliance. On Action hands it adds curiosity, and a pride in knowledge and achievement. On Emotional hands it is a stabilizing force which adds depth of intellect,

and on the Mental hand it will manifest as a love of change
and challenge.

KEY WORDS: LEARNING, DOING

RADIAL LOOP

This is an unusual print, and is considered a lucky one.
It is characterized by a true looped fingerprint, with the loop
seeming to enter from the thumb side of the hand, looping
at the little finger side, and then streaking back outward
toward the thumb. The looped section may appear to have
a tiny kernel inside, or it may have none at all.

These prints indicate strong motivation or self-direction.
You can cut your job out for yourself, set your own pace,
and do it all your own way.

There will be something unusual about how this person
perceives things; others might consider this personality to
have a "wild mind." This print typically indicates keen
visual perception; it is easier for this person to remember
what he has seen rather than what he has heard. Learning
from television would be easy. He may be able to describe
a scene, a person, a place, or landscape purely from memory, a good many years after he has seen the original.

In the index finger, the print adds keen perception and a
desire for truth. When on the ring finger, you gain the
perception of form and color in an artistic sense. A flower
garden might hold your entire attention for hours—just
drinking in the colors.

It also adds to the personality an ability to discover the
hidden patterns and cycles within what seems to be reality.
There may be an urge to explore religion, mysticism, or the
unusual to find answers to questions that nag at you. It
signifies a restless mind, always asking who, what, why,
and how.

On Technical hands, it adds great ability to perceive and understand. Mental and Emotional hands are already perceptive in their basic nature, and this loop/arch fingerprint will add to and support this perceptivity. On Action hands, it adds a genius for fast understanding and an intense craving for more information.

It is an unusual, rare print; perhaps only 10 percent of hands will have one or more, and the placement is almost always on the index fingertip.

KEY WORDS: QUESTING, SEEKING

PEACOCK FEATHER

This fingerprint is a third type of loop formation. It has a tiny bull's-eye right in the center of the looped portion. When printed, it looks exactly like the end of a peacock's feather with its blue-green central eye. It indicates a far-seeing individual, who has a positive attitude toward the future.

This print is associated with a flair for color and design. You may be involved with many people, all of whom respect your personality and brilliant mind. You are a person who will work toward a goal, which is probably a creative or artistic one; but whatever you are doing, it will be done with your own particular touch.

It has nothing to do with fate or fortune, but it adds dimension to the personality and indicates a person who is using *all* of his or her attributes.

KEY WORDS: DISTINCTIVE, ARTISTIC

DOUBLE LOOP

Depending on which finger sports this very complex print, it can be an asset or a possible liability. In some cases, obviously when associated with other factors, it may indicate a sociopathic personality. On most hands, the pattern signifies the type of mind that can adapt to challenges and changes, and withstand the difficulties of the future as well.

People with this print have minds on a different track than most. Double loops are found on the hands of persons who double-think, seem slow to make decisions, are inconsistent and changeable, and who may give the impression that they are living on some other plane of existence, for the subconscious mind is active and quite dominant at times.

Double loop

If this print appears on your hand in childhood, you may have lived in a fantasy world, had an "invisible" friend or companion. You may have had problems separating reality from the abstract or fantasy, for the exigencies of real life do not fit your ideals of what the world *should* be. This gap between reality and unreality may result in retreat into a completely fantasy-oriented existence, most usually in childhood or adolescence; and the double-looped print may create a personality that can be at times considered a pathological liar. But consideration, compassion, and perhaps therapy can help the individual sort the real from the imaginary.

Oddly, the double loop can be very constructive, and may be found in people who gravitate toward dramatic careers, such as ballerinas, choreographers, orators, and authors.

KEY WORDS: INCONSISTENT, CHANGEABLE, STORYTELLERS

OTHER PRINT FORMATIONS

There are several print formations which you will find that don't seem to fit into any of the major categories. These are referred to as "accidentals," and the way to find out what they represent is to ask questions and listen carefully to the answers.

Like the other facets of the hand, a very complete character analysis can be done with no more than the fingerprints.

Just to test yourself, locate some FBI fliers at the local post office and check out the fingerprints. You'll find the results fascinating if you compare the prints with the crimes these people may have committed.

PATTERNS ON PALMS

Most hands contain two loop formations on the palm. These patterns are generally somewhat larger than the patterns on the fingertips, and can be seen in a very good light. They show to their best effect, however, in an inked handprint.

In general, these patterns, which are present at birth, represent patterns of thinking and behavior in the personality. Hand analysts feel there is strong evidence that these palm markings have direct connection to the hereditary factors of the DNA (code gene).

These patterns have also taken on significance in scientific and medical research; for instance, Dr. Milton Alter, at the

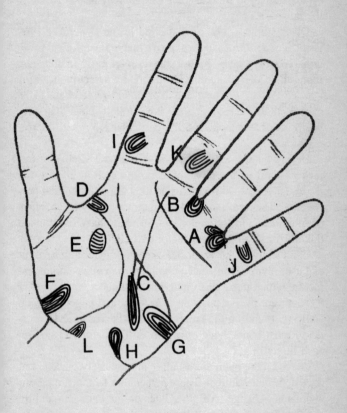

A. Humor
B. Common sense
C. Memory
D. Courage
E. Musical
F. Response
G. Genetic
H. Humanitarian
I. Charisma
J. Sexuality
K. Ownership
L. Rythym

Minneapolis VA Hospital, has found that a displaced tri-radius (junction) of skin lines can identify heart disease in the newborn baby.

Other studies, such as that cited in the December 1969 issue of *Scientific American*, prove that many physical problems can be diagnosed by palmar markings. In my own research, a loop formation identified as a defect in the DNA was proved by German and Norwegian researchers to be exactly that. Moreover, they have found more than fifty positions of this loop, and the particular DNA birth defect it denotes.

Unfortunately, although this type of research has tremendous value, there has been no research at all into the meanings of the skin patterns as they affect individual personality. The traditional field of palmistry, as well as gypsy palm readers and fortune-tellers, seems to have overlooked this immensely important factor entirely.

Hand analysis, however, takes each of them into account and uses them to construct a complete map of psychological factors which make each individual unique.

There are twelve possible skin loops and patterns which could be found on the hand. Fortunately, for analysis purposes most hands have only two on the palm and one on each fingertip.

Loops on the palm are usually very precisely placed, and have definite meanings. These personality factors are inborn and cannot change. All other lines on the hand can and do change, but the skin patterns never do.

Each of the palmar loops has its own special meaning, and adds its own influence to the total person.

THE COMMON LOOPS

A. The Humor Loop. In all polls regarding qualities that are wanted in a possible mate or lover a sense of humor is the most desirable. There are a number of types of humor, from dry wit to clowning. Some hands have loops that indicate a sense of humor, which suggests that you will find amusement in almost everything.

Your own brand of humor is specifically yours, and the loop, its position, or its absence will indicate into which category it falls.

This loop is always found between the ring and little fingers.

Placement directly between fingers indicates a normally functioning sense of humor. If you have it, it indicates you find fun in a wide range of things.

Placement slightly under ring finger indicates people who may have a slightly offbeat sense of humor. They may find mainstream humor boring and tiresome, most stand-up comics irritating, and whimsical things of their own choosing at which to laugh. It's best to avoid making this type the butt of practical jokes as they would be likely to backfire.

Placement beneath the ring finger is indicative of a person not amused by jokes at the expense of others; however such things as bloopers or misprinted headlines could be hilarious.

The absence of the loop does *not* mean a lack of humor. But without this loop, humor may be very individual. In rare cases it is completely missing. An enlarged loop which reaches deep into the palm may indicate a person who regards all of life as some huge joke. Generally speaking, the shorter the loop, the more superficial the sense of humor or the type of entertainment enjoyed. Tiny loops sometimes indicate enjoyment of pratfall humor and slapstick. The extremely tiny loop may, if less than a quarter of an inch in length, suggest the practical joker—humor on a basic level. This loop size is extremely rare.

When the loop is absent, but an odd L-shaped pattern appears between the two fingers, the sense of humor is likely to be of a very individual sort. Those with this formation prefer less obvious types of comedy. Like those with the very sideways-displaced loop, they are resentful of any joke made at the expense of another. Their reaction to this type of humor could be sarcasm or even anger.

A whorl here would be exceptional, but if found between the ring and little finger it would indicate a person whose outward reactions are so completely buried in the subconscious that he or she may seem to be entirely humorless. Whorls are the indicators of concentration, wherever they appear.

A. Ego Loop. This formation is related to the index finger, which is also commonly associated with the ego. It loops toward that finger, often completely across the bulge below the ring finger.

If this loop appears, the person is likely to be very self-conscious, and may find it an effort to be more outgoing and less self-absorbed.

B. The Commonsense Loop. This marking is found between the middle finger and the ring finger. If it is there, you are likely to be gifted with fine common sense, or what is known as plain old horse sense.

It also indicates a personality which feels responsibility toward others, not necessarily just friends or family.

Doctors, medical researchers, nurses, social workers, and leaders of community groups and charities may have this loop on their palms.

G. The Ulnar Loop. I was recently informed by a group of Norwegian analysts that my original assessment of this loop was correct.

It can and does relate to the genetic or DNA structure of the body and mind. Its placement has been found to indicate a great many DNA defects or idiosyncrasies. On the hands of a newborn, it can help physicians to discover what type of help the child may need.

It is a rare pattern. Among the less startling features this loop indicates, it marks one whose life is enriched through its sensitivity to the world of nature and the outdoors. It might be found on the hands of an avid gardener, an animal lover, a professional conservationist, a beekeeper, an animal breeder, or someone involved in dealing with the world of nature, perhaps a national park ranger.

In general, the higher up on the hand it appears, the better. If it is found almost at the middle of the hand, it more likely signifies that the person is an outdoors lover, with all of the other traits—hardihood, simplicity—that go with a feeling for nature.

If it is found more than two-thirds from the base of the fingers, it may be an indication of some unusual attribute of the subconscious mind. Since it is seen to enter from the subconscious area of the hand, it may indicate one who is motivated basically by the workings of the subconscious, rather than the conscious mind. This might mean a poet, a writer of fiction, an artist, a decorator, or a metaphysician of some kind. One's interests will be guided by imagination and the workings of the inner mind.

Finding it very low on the hand, very near the wrist, the loop might be considered only in balance with the rest of the personality and what has happened during one's lifetime. It may represent some medical problems, which we will cover in Chapter 7.

For those having the loop anywhere on the hand, it is likely that being outdoors or traveling into wild regions of the country are experiences they love. This can be a very supporting aspect, and may enrich an otherwise ordinary life immeasurably.

C. The Memory Loop.

This is the largest loop. It has several directions and forms, but it is found running alongside or entwined with the head line, and for a good reason—it indicates how good your memory capacity may be.

In fact, it signifies an almost perfect memory, sometimes known as photographic.

The mind is like a computer, in that it stores *everything* you see and do—the people and places you see—even the sounds you hear and the scents you smell. If you punch the right button this computer-storage memory will obligingly bring back the original impression in full detail.

As people age, much of this storage seems to vanish, leaving them wondering why they were looking in the refrigerator for their pencil, when it was really the shoe polish that they wanted. If the loop appears full-size upon the hand, it is likely one will never suffer from this scrambling effect.

The smaller the loop, and the closer to the head line, the less imaginative the memory. If the loop dips deep into the side of the palm, or down into the lower outside edge of the palm, then the memory will not only dredge up the fact one is trying to remember, but will supply everything associated with it as well. With a small loop, the memory is less retentive, but still very good.

H. The Inspiration Loop.

The presence of such a loop on the hand seems to add a very special quality to life—that of inspiration.

These people have a great love for color and for music, and can become inspired by a certain piece of music, a poem, or a favorite book—a particular style or work of art, or sometimes even by contact with a special type of person.

People having this loop have, in addition, the ability to pass on this inspirational quality, almost by contagious enthusiasm, to those who surround them. They draw people to them as if by magic, and they may never know the secret of the appeal.

Such a person can be a natural leader, guiding by inspiring those he or she leads. It is an extremely lucky loop to have, and can be used to great advantage in marriage, parenting, and in most areas of contact with those one meets, lives, or works with.

One with a long tip on the ring finger and the little finger should be a teacher or guide, even if only in such a job as a scout leader or sports coach. If the long tip appears on the ring finger only, the gift is in working with other people and helping them to change the negative to the positive. On the little finger only, one can inspire others by the power of language, become a public speaker, or a singer whose voice captivates an audience.

This loop would be expected to have been present on such charismatic individuals as John Kennedy, Martin Luther King, the author Napoleon Hill, or great religious leaders such as Dr. Norman Vincent Peale or Robert Schuller.

Radio and television stars may also have this loop, and it might be expected to be on the hands of Johnny Carson or Oprah Winfrey, even if it is small and barely visible.

It is a powerful indication on the hand, even if it is rare to find one.

The inspiration loop also has a relationship to the religious feelings of its owners, and they are often of the type for whom formal, complicated forms of religion will not "take." All aspects of religion must be explored, until they discover something they can *feel* is right for them.

Emotion and intellect operate hand-in-hand for those who

have this loop, and both must be satisfied before they will accept anything.

People with this loop may find that they are satisfied and wonderfully inspired by the beauty of a winter sunset, a quiet lake, or forest pool—the wonders of nature, and sometimes, the wonders of mankind.

They will also choose and send greeting cards on any pretext to everyone to whom they feel close; and the style of Christmas card they choose will be unusual and meaningful.

This is a rare but extremely beneficial loop to have.

E. The Musical or Rhythm Loop. Closely akin to rhythm, the presence of this loop often denotes an almost magical attraction to anything that utilizes rhythm of sound, body, or mind.

With this loop, a person will perhaps be a fine dancer; one who excels at some sport, who sings, writes music, or plays an instrument; a tennis player or artist.

Lines of form and rhythmic tempos are their forte, and they will be found living in an extremely decorative setting, of their own choosing.

This loop is found on the hands of those who love Art Deco or Art Nouveau, because of the flowing lines of Nouveau, or the angular stylization of Art Deco. They will surround themselves with one or the other, or, in rare cases, both.

If you have the loop on your hand, run one finger down the outside of your thumb. If you find a "bump" just below the thumb, indicating an enlargement of this hidden knuckle, you should seek out which of the rhythm-oriented areas of creativity is best for you, and pursue it.

If the loop appears on the hand of a child, effort should be made to test his or her aptitudes while young, so that education and training will be given at the proper time to develop them fully.

It is a fairly common loop, and a promising one.

People with this loop also have a strong fascination with music, which may only result in listening and enjoying it; or even to *using* it to create or change a mood. If feeling depressed, those who have this loop can turn on a radio or a CD player and actually *change* their mood to an uplifted one.

The intricate rhythms of sports are also second nature to you if you have this loop on the hand, and many famous players of tennis, soccer, or baseball have had it; as have many persons of Olympic-quality swimming, diving, or gymnastics.

All of these abilities require the use and mastery of body rhythm and synchronicity of mind and body. If you have this loop, your life can be satisfying and dramatic. It is a mistake to have this loop and not develop it.

If this loop appears on your recessive hand only, then it may represent inherited talent you may not be aware of. Do explore your secret dreams and wishes, then take a class or training to develop the talent or ability they suggest.

F. The Response Loop.

People with the response loop on the hand will be strongly affected by both people and events.

This loop is quite rare, but will be found on 4 percent of hands in one form or another, often on men and women of Mediterranean heritage. If your forebears came from Greece, Cyprus, Italy, or Turkey, it is possible that you may have this loop on one or both hands.

People who have it are capable of intense response to their surroundings, music, sunsets or sunrises, weather "fronts" or barometric changes, and most of all, to those with whom they interact. This loop belongs to those who are extremely changeable or chameleonlike in reaction to stimuli.

When in a group that is serious or intent, they too will be earnest and concentrating, listening closely. If the group is in a party mood, they will correspondingly find themselves joining in with laughter and enjoyment as well.

If this loop is on one's hand, even the physical surroundings are of extreme importance, for the emotional state depends upon the harmony of color, fabric, and furnishings. In a dismal or dirty place, such people feel uncomfortable and depressed. If the place is clean and tasteful, they feel at home. If it is palatial, with fine sculpture and paintings on the walls, they may feel either awed or overwhelmed.

For people having the loop, care should be taken to spend time only in places where they feel comfortable. They should also avoid any aspect of confinement. An extended stay on a submarine or in a jail could seem intolerable, and caves may make them extremely uncomfortable, no matter how dramatic they may seem. There is a slight claustrophobic aspect to this loop, and they should be cautious about getting into a situation they cannot control or leave at will.

Associating only with people who have a positive attitude is also wise, as nothing will get one down more than to be with people who are morose, unhappy, or angry.

If you find this loop on your hand, do not consider it a threatening aspect. It is not, unless conditions find you boxed in or unable to exert control over where you are and what is happening. For those whose jobs require them to deal with the public, or to speak, act, sing, or do comedy it can be a very positive asset; for it will enable them to feel the mood and response of their audience, since the loop is associated with empathy.

In marriage or family life one may seem almost psychic, able to respond to the moods and feelings of mate, children, or relatives. It may almost seem the person knows what others are going to say before they say it.

Positive benefits of this loop can outweigh the negative.

D. The Courage Loop. It might seem more common for this loop to appear on male hands, but it does appear on many female hands as well. Women who have a courage loop are adventurous and willing to "try anything once."

As children, the boys were mischiefmakers, but intensely bright, willing, generous, and adventurous. Females with this loop will recognize themselves in these attributes as well, for they would have been known as tomboys.

The loop adds forcefulness to the personality, as well as a sense of fearlessness. The person having it on the hand is a natural leader, resourceful and inventive. If something can't be done in the normal way, he or she will find a way to do it anyway.

Resilient and positive, this is the type that, when faced with misfortune, bad luck, or adversity, will not find someone else to blame, but will search diligently and resourcefully for a way out of the situation.

Having formed an emotional opinion about something or developed an intellectual conviction, they will defend it to the bitter end—stubborn, yes, but loyal and faithful as well. They will support whatever they truly believe with all the time, energy, wit, and strength they possess.

The loop adds strength of character, even in an otherwise weak hand.

Having this loop doesn't mean the person is argumentative or vainly combative, but it does mean that he or she will spend a lifetime finding causes worth fighting for—and fighting for them. It is an indication of an individual with deep inner conviction and perseverance.

A most interesting loop, but rare, it may be difficult to

see unless the thumb is spread completely away from the fingers. It may be small or hard to find, especially if the owner plays golf, tennis, or any sport which involves holding an instrument between thumb and fingers.

If it is found on another's hand, it would be interesting to learn just what that person likes to do, or what unusual things he or she has tried during the lifetime.

H. The Humanitarian Loop.

Perhaps the rarest of all the loops, one would expect the owner of the hand to belong to an organization like Greenpeace, an environmental coalition, or the Peace Corps. This has been found on persons in ordinary professions whose aspirations were high, although opportunity has limited their choices.

If you have this loop, you may tend to put your parents, your mate, or your children upon a pedestal, thinking them perfect—and then suddenly discover that they, like all humanity, have problems, worries, personal idiosyncrasies, and failures—in other words, it's not a perfect world.

This discovery may cause disillusionment or depression. It usually occurs in childhood or adolescence, and inevitably ends in their being more understanding, wiser individuals.

On a strong hand, it might produce an idealist, a person who works in his or her own way for peace and the uplifting of humanity. On a weak hand, it could produce a cynical, embittered misfit.

If you discover this loop on your hand, it may be profitable to study motivation psychology and positive-thinking techniques. These would give you a handle on your own reactions, and perhaps a more positive direction to utilize some of your humanitarian instincts. If you do no more than make out a check for one of the environmental-crisis groups, you will be doing your part to help make a better world.

Rare and precious, this loop can signify a grandeur of its own in the person who is lucky enough to have it.

The Royal Loop. (not shown) This unusual loop is found on less than 2 percent of hands. It is known as the royal loop because it was supposedly frequently found on the hands of persons with royal ancestors.

I have observed this loop only four times, and in none of these cases was I able to confirm that the individual's forebears wore a crown. This would, in fact, make little sense, as royalty is not a physical state and would have little effect upon the mind of an unborn child.

There has been recent medical evidence suggesting that the loop is found on the hands of individuals who may have some chromosomal abnormalities.

It is true that this loop is sometimes found on the palm of a person who has an extremely overpowering presence, and this may be why it was given such a distinctive designation.

Unfinished Loops. (see G on p. 67.) There are some loop formations that do not look "complete," and may appear as only a partial formation, perhaps on the edge of the hand, or a finger's lower segment.

There was such a loop on the hand of the great psychiatrist Carl Jung. It appears to have been a humor loop, but it is incomplete. This could indicate that his sense of humor was offbeat, or submerged by the gravity of his research into human psychology.

If you have such an unfinished loop, you should assign it the same value as a complete looping formation, but it may be somewhat less effective in your life.

UNUSUAL SKIN PATTERNS

Although most hands will contain two or, at most, three skin pattern loops, there are some which add one or more of the less common identifiable group. Some of these are loops, but others are whorls, swirls, and one is totally enclosed by an oval line just like the back end of a bee. These are:

A)   The Reverse "L" Formation
B)   Interdigital Whorls
C)   The "Bee" of Music
D)   Arched Formations
E)   Double Loops
F)   Charisma Loop on Index Finger
G)   Sexuality Factor Loop on Little Finger
H)   Arched or Depressed Skin Patterns

A. THE REVERSE L

Between ring and little finger, where the loop of memory is often found, there is sometimes a clearly marked "L", but reversed as if in a mirror. This angular formation signifies a fairly unusual sort of humor, to say the least. Those who have it are intrigued by the patterns of human communication, and find humor in human behavior. The best stand-up comedians often have this "L" on their hands. They find humor in the everyday affairs of life and living— their mates, their parents, and their dogs and cats. Often, these are the best and funniest of comedians.

The reverse "L" is less often found between the middle finger and the ring finger. This pattern is not related to common sense at all, but indicates a restless mind, never satisfied, and one always searching for truth or personal

Unusual Skin Patterns

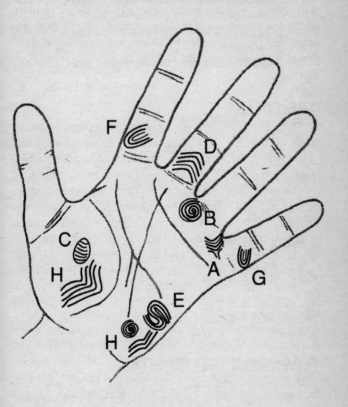

fulfillment. This type seeks mental or intellectual stimulation and may often continue to pursue formal education throughout the entire life span.

They may be considered aloof or "stuck up" by those who do not understand them, for emotional happiness can only be achieved after personal fulfillment has been reached. This was one of the driving forces behind the tragedy of Marilyn Monroe, who wished to be a dramatic actress and not a sex goddess.

It's a difficult placement and the person must learn how to handle it.

THE COLLAR

The collar is difficult to see with the eye, impossible on a photocopy, but if you are taking a handprint with ink, you can look for a series of bolder skin pattern lines which appear immediately beneath one or more of the fingers.

This collar has the effect of lessening the force of all the talents and skills that finger represents. It's like a cord that strangles off the areas of life covered by the finger sections.

If you have this, you will easily see that the lines are much deeper and more visible than the rest of the skin patterns on the hand, standing out distinctly. If this collar is crossed with vertical lines, it is possible that the constricting effect is being overcome. It is interesting to note these collars and just what parts of the life they may be restricting.

B. WHORLS INTERDIGITAL

It is rare to find such a skin pattern, but if you see a bull's-eye located just beneath or in the space between the bases of two fingers, this would be considered an interdigital whorl. Wherever you find it, it represents concentration on the areas of life indicated by those fingers.

For instance, if found in the area where the commonsense

loop would be, it would indicate that you might be a person whose devotion to duty could be excessive, causing you to leave no job undone, or no stone unturned in the search for truth.

You might be someone who relies entirely upon logical thinking, like *Star Trek*'s Dr. Spock.

In place of the humor loop, it would indicate a person who refuses to take anything seriously, and who seems to have a lot more fun in life than most of us do. If channeled into writing, this loop could assure you of fame in producing extremely funny books, articles, television shows, or movies.

On the lower outside edge of the hand, in the area of imagination, it indicates a person with what could be called a "wild mind," bubbling with creativity.

It also may indicate a person whose emotional moods are extremely intense. If you have this whorl it would be safe to say that you are an extremely unusual person.

On the fleshy mound beneath the thumb, a whorl would be so uncommon that it might change any or all of the aspects of the hand. Whorls represent concentration, and in this position would indicate a person whose concentration on self is all-absorbing. One will probably act and react purely on the basis of how one feels toward oneself, and perhaps toward others as well. Be certain that you are looking at a bull's-eye whorl and not a "Bee" when you find an unusual pattern on this mount. A bull's-eye has concentric circles, one inside the other, just like a target.

C. THE "BEE" OF MUSIC

Looking closely at the skin just inside the bottom of the thumb, you may find a small oval, no more than ¼- to ½-inch wide, with tiny, curved lines inside it. These lines will go in the same direction, but will probably be at an angle completely different from normal skin patterns, which would usually curve gently around from the top of the thumb to the base of the palm. In fact, they are often at right angles to these normal lines.

When this is seen, it indicates an individual who has a genius for music and harmony. It is strongest with an oval line completely enclosing it, but may be found just as if floating on the curving lines, but in a completely different direction.

The reason we call it the Bee is that it looks just like the back of a honeybee.

Wherever it is seen, and in whichever form, it indicates a strong musical talent. Some who have it can compose music, while others can play instruments by ear with no training at all. It indicates a person who can almost "feel" music, and to whom it has deep meaning.

Children who possess this marking should be helped and encouraged to develop their talents. When a hand with this marking comes into contact with a musical instrument or receives training in music theory, the rest will come naturally.

D. TENTED ARCH ON THUMB MOUNT

While the lines on the lower portion of the hand toward the thumb are usually moving in a soft, sweeping curve, there is an unusual formation in which these curving lines suddenly peak to one side.

It is also related to music, but rather than a career indication, it would denote the person who just enjoys music. Singing might be one way to express this, or playing piano or another keyboard instrument by ear. Owners of this mark usually admit that they love music, and many of them sing, if only in the shower and for themselves alone. Or they might be found singing in a church choir or barbershop quartet. This formation is often found on the hands of per-

sons of Irish or Scottish descent. Many country music per-
formers have it.

Markings on the Mount of Imagination

E. DOUBLE LOOPS

Most outstanding of the formations found on the fleshy lower
portion of the palm, known as the mount of imagination,
is the double loop.

This is a skin pattern discovered and classified during my
own research. On the mount of imagination, it indicates an
inability to separate the real and unreal aspects of life.

We grow from children believing in the Easter bunny,
the tooth fairy, and Santa Claus to an adulthood where such
beings cease to exist. This is called the evolution of intellect.

People with this double loop may be living in a world of
their own, perhaps one constructed in the depths of their
own minds, or in a world seen through the rose-colored
glasses of the idealist. It can be a very comfortable world
in which to exist, where reality becomes spangled with the
stardust of the unreal, and nothing can be as bad as it seems.

Far from retreating into withdrawal, these people build a
special porthole through which they view everything. It
might seem that this is a false view, but since the result for
those who can do it is happiness, the result may justify the
means. More beneficially, the loop may give the person a
childlike quality of innocence, a nostalgic longing, and a
constant search for new and different things to learn, to do,
or to experience.

If this double-looping skin pattern is combined with a
crooked, twisted little finger, it may result in the inability
to tell the truth. This is because the overlooping within the
imagination may keep them from separating truth from fiction. Those having this skin pattern can convince themselves
so firmly that their belief is true, they will unwittingly or

actively try to convince others that the sky is falling—the Chicken Little syndrome. Because of this, they often become lonely and feel alienated from humanity, or form a firm conviction that they must be superior beings, as they are the only ones who can see what's really going on. Sometimes these people are called "martyrs," not in the religious sense, but because they make a career of feeling hurt when others don't agree with their conclusions.

If you have this marking, remember that it is extremely rare, and may be much less effective on an Action, a Mental, or a Technical hand. In fact, on these hands it may signify a fantasy writer, an inspired artist, a professional storyteller, or an inventor of wondrous talent.

It is most awkward on the Emotional hand, where it may have caused real problems in childhood and adolescence, but have been conquered in adulthood.

Wherever it is found, it represents a type of double-think that makes the mind an unusual, perhaps eccentric one.

Whorl. As stated previously, this is an indication of a vivid and creative imagination. It can be a positive asset, and if you have it, your life is certain to be exciting.

Imagination is the keystone, and career choices are infinite.

Tented Arch. If the skin pattern on this part of the hand shows a swooping curve coming down from the area of the index finger, this is normal. If, however, it has a place where the pattern seems to be interrupted and pulled sideways, then it is an indication of something unusual in the depths of the subconscious. This type may be able to use the mind to do things other people cannot duplicate.

If there is a forked ending on the head line as well, it could mean a gift for journalism and writing. If there is a long tip on the little finger, there will be a genius for communication.

This skin pattern also seems to have something to do with the memory process, enabling the person to remember statistics with ease, for instance, Lou Gehrig's batting average.

It is a positive marking, and should denote an exceptional personality.

F. CHARISMA LOOP

Found on base of index finger, this loop indicates that you can draw people to you effortlessly, you are a natural leader, and you often inspire total loyalty in those who believe in you.

G. SEXUALITY FACTOR LOOP

Finding this loop on the hand of a bride or a groom may be the brightest spot in any wedding. It indicates a person whose masculinity or feminity is strong, generous and not inhibited. Although people with this loop may be faithful and monogamous, they seem to draw ''friends'' of the opposite sex to them irresistibly. Fortunately, these relationships will be platonic friendships and not romantic relationships. Rare, but interesting, this loop signifies an almost magnetically attractive personality.

H. ARCHED FORMATION

Found on any finger segment, this highly arched formation indicates an attitude of optimism in the area of life represented by that finger section.

In every hand there are markings and skin patterns which are completely individualistic, and which belong only to you. Even the hands of identical or mirror twins have differences, and one may have a flair for art, while the other cannot draw a straight line. These special markings on your hand are pieces of the jigsaw puzzle that is you and you alone. Each of them adds some piece of personality and color to your character.

4

FASCINATING FINGERS

For decades, palmists, and experts on the hand have told us that the thumb is the most important part of the hand after the palm itself, and yet they never said *why* it was so important. Hand analysis has found that it is indeed of great significance if only because it is the largest of the digits and an indicator of the will, the response factor, and one's athletic prowess.

A powerful, well-balanced thumb can lift a hand out of the ordinary into the category of special personalities.

The fingers and thumb can give a very accurate, clear idea about the person, even without the inked prints, or the rest of the hand. After a radio show on CBS, a listener misunderstood instructions and just drew around her hand rather than making a print for me. I was able to do a very complete analysis for her with only that. You can imagine her surprise.

FINGER SIZES

In the first chapter we discussed the length of fingers on the hands in deciding how to type them. In general, the longer the fingers the more patient the person, while shorter fingers hint at impatience and restlessness.

All of the fingers on a hand will not be the same length, and the relative sizes of each can be important.

LARGE ROUND FINGERS

These are usually found on the Technical and possibly the Action hand, and indicate the person who possesses energy and prefers to think while on the go. Anyone who has ever had trouble trying to meditate, or sit still listening to a lecture or a long sermon, may have this type of fingers all across the hand.

THIN LONG FINGERS

Usually, these fingers belong to the person with a patient, thoughtful, less excitable personality, and a calm outlook on life. They may be slightly more inclined to negativity than those with larger fingers, but a large, strong thumb can lift this indication into a more balanced view of the world.

FINGER BALANCE

In deciding balance, the two most critical fingers are the index and the ring finger. These may be measured from the base where they join the palm, or from the photocopy or inkprint.

Often the index finger is longer than the ring finger. When it is obviously longer, it indicates leadership potential, individuals who are good at executing projects and performing any job that requires power and authority. The person has a strong presence, and will stand out in any crowd, if he or she wishes to do so.

If the ring finger is noticeably longer, the person is a technician, able to understand people and machines and to plan in advance. Less spontaneous, he or she may prefer to be the power *behind* the throne, and let those with the long index finger take the lead.

One aspect of this difference was seen in the hands of the astronaut team that made the first Moon landing in 1969. The pilots of the command module that made the landing both had longer index fingers, while the backup pilots who stayed in orbit around the satellite had the longer ring fingers of the born technician. Naturally, all astronauts are competent technicians, but it was interesting to see that the long-index owners actually stepped onto the Moon and gained eternal fame.

Take a look at the hands of your favorite actor, actress, or politician. Watch until they show their hands, which most of those in the eye of the public often do, and notice which of the "balance" fingers is longer. It may surprise you.

If there is no measurable or discernible difference in the length of these two fingers, then the personality is a well-balanced one, capable of both leading and following, depending on the stimulus.

LITTLE FINGERS

Little fingers are naturally shorter than all the rest. The important factor is not *how* short, but how *low-set* the digit is on the hand. (*See figure, p. 78.*)

A very low-set little finger indicates that you were probably quite shy when a child, nonadventurous, preferring to conduct your own secret exploits in your imagination.

As an adult, you are still not one to take the initiative in interpersonal relationships, but are capable of a long-lasting and faithful friendship. You still have secrets, and wild horses couldn't drag them out of you.

Some *extremely* low-set little fingers could indicate inherited tendencies to neurosis, but a strong, well-balanced hand will outweigh this. On a weak hand, it is a definite possibility, and should be explored along with the major lines and skin patterns to find the problem.

A high-set little finger which is just slightly lower in the hand than the rest of the fingers is the sign of the bold and risk-loving chance-taker. This type may like to gamble in one or another area of life, and presents a much more prominent personality than the hand with a low-set finger.

In love such persons tend to be affectionate and want to show it, and cannot abide a secret (but can keep one if they have to). They are full of ideas and possibly expert at some form of communication.

Usually free of phobias, they may be overconfident at times and possibly a bit careless.

While the individual with the low-set little finger always remembers birthdays and other important occasions with a thoughtful card, the higher-set finger will cheerfully send out a "sorry I forgot" card, probably with a generous gift.

A balanced little finger should be approximately ¼ inch below the level of the others at the base where it joins the palm. A very high or very low finger will be obvious even without any measurement involved. If it is very high or very low, adjust the interpretations given above.

THE THUMB— KEY TO POWER

In the lore of the hand, the thumb sections were divided into only two sections, tip and base, while the truth is that

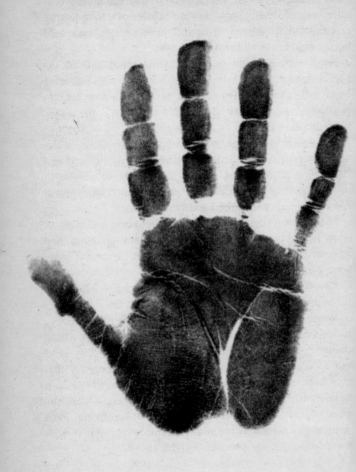

**High-set little finger
Long lower thumb section**

the thumb, like all the other fingers, has three sections. The top section has been assigned to willpower and determination; the "bottom" (actually the middle section) to reasoning ability. These indications are, however, only partially correct. The three sections of the thumb are:

Tip: Instinct, intuition, willpower, and grit or stick-to-itiveness

Middle: Logic, reason, judgment, common sense or horse sense

Bottom: Strength of personality, ability to act or carry plans through, the major aspects of life and ability to control not only oneself but one's reactions in general

In the past, the lowest part of the thumb, actually extending down to the wrist, was considered to be the "mount of Venus" and if it was strong and highly puffed, one would be considered a hot-blooded lover, sensual and overbearing.

This portion of the thumb has no connection to the planet Venus, however, but does have a direct connection to strength, stamina, self-control, and responses to life and living.

If the joint beneath the two top portions of the thumb is well-defined, even showing a prominent bump at that knuckle, the person is liable to have a strong temper, quick to erupt and hard to control. It is, however, the fast-burning type which is quickly over and if you can bite your lip—count to ten—or practice whatever means you can find to keep from blowing up, you will find it a much easier job to live with this "temper" bump.

If the thumb flows smoothly into the curve leading toward the wrist, with no noticeable enlargement of the second knuckle, it is likely that you are slow to anger, usually a peacemaker and, in fact, you may become so distressed

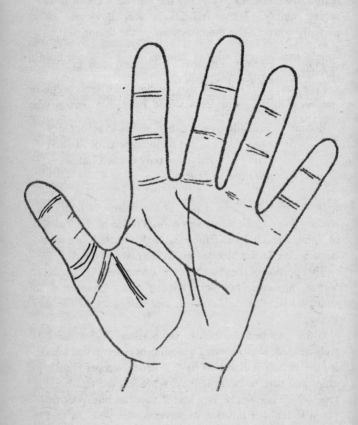

Special Thumb Markings

when people around you are upset or angry that you will have to leave the room.

A very small bulge would indicate a normal temper, easy to control.

A deep depression at this spot, unless caused by arthritis, might indicate one who is slow to anger but will hold a grudge for a long time.

The base of the thumb may be flat, with little bulge or puffiness in the palm. This would indicate a person who isn't weak, but lacks some of the vivacity and sense of excitement of life. If the lower section is thin and hard, the person may be getting less out of life than one could wish, and may be subject to some nagging little physical problems.

Too much puffiness in the base of the thumb might indicate a person who possesses much vitality, participates in life with zest and strong enjoyment, and is usually found in the thick of the action.

They are strongly interested in themselves, those around them, and events.

If the thumb base is soft and the finger sinks into it when pressed, there may be a tendency to lack of energy or a possible problem with water retention. Some women have this problem once a month, while others may experience it more regularly.

If the section is firm and resilient, the individual is just as firm in personal convictions, yet willing to compromise if necessary. Energy is high (blood pressure may be as well), and this type likes to get involved with a multitude of things and will always be surrounded with people and projects. The temperament is easy-going, friendly, and optimistic.

If the section is hard and thin, this type may be suffering from events in the past, which keeps them from being outgoing, and they may resent the fact that they did not receive enough education when young, or think they did not. They may be subject to low blood pressure, iron deficiency, and lack of energy. This can often be alleviated by enrolling in interesting clubs, classes, or some form of educational enrichment that will fulfill the need to achieve self-improvement.

THE INTENSITY LINE

Often this lowest section of the thumb is deeply creased by a diagonal line which may be deeper than any other line on the hand. On a print, it might show as a completely white streak cutting across the pad toward the lifeline which encircles the base of the thumb. If this mark appears on the palm, it denotes a person with unusual intensity. Whatever such a type does is done with energy, wit, and style. They will dive into projects and give them all they've got; then turn to another with the same eagerness for experience and fulfillment. (*See figure, p.80*)

They will love deeply, enjoy music and theater, read books, solve puzzles, and usually love a mystery.

Altogether, this intensity line is a very interesting mark to have on any hand. It is not uncommon, and adds spice to any life.

THE MIDDLE THUMB SECTION

Usually crossed by many lines, this thumb section indicates ability to use logic and reason. Analytical thinkers, these individuals have often found that their instinctual feelings have been more reliable than logic and there may be a mental battle between what they know to be true, and what they feel.

The more lines, the more often this happens. If the thumb section is thin, the ability to follow logical lines of thought may not be strong, and instinctual action will rule.

If it is approximately the same size and strength as the tip, then a fine balance is struck between logic, reasoning ability, and the proddings of intuition and instinct.

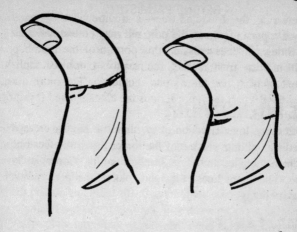

**Long Tip—
Lacks Reason and Logic**

**Short Tip—
Little Will-Power**

Both aspects of the mind can be used to good effect. It is a very productive thumb when this balance is present.

THUMB TIPS

This portion of the thumb is normally rounded and feels resilient or "bouncy" to the touch. The nail may lie flat or project at an angle.

A distinct outward bend from the base of the thumb section outward, or beginning at the bottom of the nail, reveals an outgoing personality, generous and appreciative of others and of what they contribute.

You are creative, multitalented, and have strong opinions. Life is a challenge to you, and you will eagerly stride forward to meet it. You are also very intuitive.

A thumb section that remains straight, in line with the middle section, shows a comfortably well-balanced person, trusting and sincere, one not inclined to take chances, but preferring the tried-and-true—a traditionalist by nature. Such a person reveres the past and may collect antiques.

Sideways lines crossing this portion of the thumb pad will indicate frustration. Circumstances block accomplishment of what one knows one should do. The more lines, and the deeper, the more serious the blockage and resulting frustration.

If these lines are echoed by the same blockages on the lower or middle section of the thumb, then the frustration is being applied from pressures in family, career, or love life. The more lines, the more blocks the personality is experiencing.

IMBALANCES

A chainlike ring appearing on the middle section of the thumb reveals a person who tries hard to act in what is felt to be the proper manner, but is not always able to accomplish this. If the chained ring is accompanied by vertical lines crossing it, then most decisions are based on intuition or a combination of feelings and what has been learned from experience. Since experience is said to be the best teacher, perhaps letting it rule one's decisions will work out more successfully than a slow, logical approach might.

If there are several rings, this is a person who is operating strictly on feelings. He may achieve success, but could never explain just how he did it.

These general rules apply also to the length and relative size of the top and middle sections as well. If a thumb is thin below and thick or puffy above, then this is one who sets out in life to follow his heart, and usually will not profit from experience—unless the knocks received are strong enough to leave bruises. Persons with this thumb will also make decisions hastily, and will often tread where angels won't. They cannot or will not see far enough ahead to become aware of dangers in any course of action. The more accentuated this imbalance is, the more reckless the owner seems to be.

Conversely, the middle section of the thumb may be wider or stronger-looking than the tip. Such a person acts only on the basis of past experience, and follows a logical train of thought and action. This thumb belongs to those who are slower to act and decide than others; and because of their active minds, may *seem* to do less than most.

If you have this thumb, you may never get many of your plans off the drawing board, because you've spotted a flaw in the idea or may have decided on the basis of past experience that whatever it is will not work. You will be fond of games.

BALANCE

A thumb which has both sections full, rounded, uncrossed by many chains or lines, and with a firm, rounded lower section will belong to a person who is sympathetic, emotionally well balanced, generous, and interested in many things or everything.

Usually a charming, intellectual person, the balanced thumb marks you as one others are happy to know and to be around. You will never lack friends or interests.

A balanced thumb can lift a weak hand to a much stronger level. If your thumb is balanced, count yourself lucky, because you really are.

FINGERS

No hand will ever have fingers with all sections balanced in the size and length of each section. It is just these differences that give you your own individuality—that mark you as different from any other person on earth.

Not only the length of the fingers, but the separate sections of each finger may tell what the individual's talents may be, what the career or vocation should be, and what strengths and weaknesses the personality and psychological makeup may comprise.

MEASURING

For fast analysis, fingers may be numbered from the tip to the palm, the tip section being number 1.

With a small 6-inch ruler, you can easily measure the length of each of the three sections. Depending on the hand type, each section will generally measure from ¾ to 1¼ inches in length.

Measure from the knuckle if possible, as this gives the true length of the section. If you are looking at an inkprint or photocopy, you may be fooled by the division lines which occur on the palm side of the hand and which may not clearly indicate the actual length. If you have nothing but a print, measure from the middle of this creased area.

If working with an actual hand, you can slip the ruler into place beside each finger and measure from palm to knuckle, then move the ruler up to that point and resume measuring. Make a note of each section's exact length as you go, such as:

Index
tip 1″
middle 1½″
bottom ¾″

Be certain that you press the tip section firmly down to get a true length, as some fingertips have the extra fleshy pad of sensitivity, which may make them look or even measure as shorter than they actually are.

Psychological Relationships

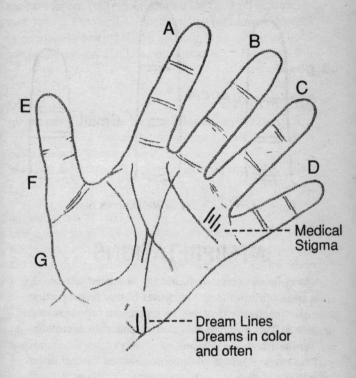

A - Index relates to the EGO
B - Middle finger relates to SUPEREGO
C - Ring finger relates to PERSONA or MASK
D - Little finger relates to ID or LIBIDO
E - Thumb tip relates to INSTINCT
F - Thumb middle relates to LOGICAL THOUGHT
G - Thumb bottom relates to WILLPOWER and
     FORCE OF PERSONALITY

The widespread little finger relates to Independence and
freedom of expression

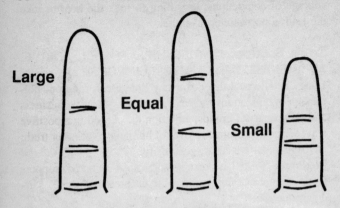

Finger Sections Vary in Relation to Size

INTERPRETATIONS

A long finger section indicates the dominant section. A short one indicates that the attributes of that finger portion are either inactive or they may be suppressed for one reason or another. This would be indicated by random lines crossing the section from side to side.

If the average lengths of finger sections on a finger differ only slightly, then a quarter-inch more or less will make that section dominant.

INDEX FINGER
Longer than Ring Finger by ½ Inch. Power; drive; leadership; ego; self-confidence; self-awareness; recognition of self as part of creation; personality projection; resilience.

Shorter than Ring Finger by ½ Inch. Lack of self-confidence; may have feelings of inferiority; self-doubt; possible lack of willpower; passivity; conformity; may lack the courage of convictions; unwilling to rock the boat or take the lead; a norm-lover; average.

Top Section. LEADERSHIP, POWER, DRIVE, AWARENESS, INTELLECT, SELF-WORTH

Long. Intellectual; talent for law; interest in religion, politics, or organizations such as Freemasons, Rotary, business and progressional groups; ambition to succeed in a positive way; seeks advancement; lover of humanity; seeks for truth; environmental concerns; generosity.

Medium. Normal interest in self; career-oriented; supportive leadership; introspective; can possess active self-determination.

Short. Usually a conformist; may lack a sense of self; one who may be afraid of either himself or of life in general; may believe in predestination or fate and that one cannot struggle against "the system."

(*Very* short. Inferiority complex; phobias; with badly chained major lines such as head or head and heart lines— paranoia or hypochondria.)

Middle Section. AMBITION, ADVANCEMENT, CAREER, IMPULSIVE, SEEKING

Long. Very ambitious; aggressive; forward-looking; may fly headlong into whatever is being studied or planned; love of advancement for its own sake; constantly on the search for self; a sign of strong individuality; intelligence; impulsiveness; true charity; interest in community betterment; strong personality factors.

Medium. Normally ambitious; interested in self-advancement; open to opportunity; willing to work hard to achieve; often self-educated.

Short. Often lacks ambition and drive; nonaggressive; not a self-starter; plods through life; may be too self-conscious; possibly drifts from one interest to another; may take advantage of others' generosity; usually has a very high opinion of himself or herself.

(*Very* long. May be power-mad; megalomaniacal; dictatorial; possess a strong sense of personal superiority whether true or not; will push others out of his or her way to the top.)

Lower Section. PRIDE, HUMANITY, EGO, DISPLAY, ACTING, HUNGER FOR RECOGNITION

Long. Warmth and generosity; affection; considerate and caring are the keynote; pride of person; love of power and attention, success and display; may have a motherlike concern for humanity; strong imagination; love of or talent for stage, acting and drama; a dramatic personality with strong loves and hates.

Medium. Caring and affectionate; will do anything to make another happy; generous and considerate; loves life and living; makes a wonderful parent.

Short. May lack sympathy for others; possibly timid or fearful; likes horror movies and books; may be superstitious; possibly a professional martyr; does not seek limelight; a follower but usually not a leader.

(*Very* long. Possible egomania; disregard of others' needs; misuse of power; a pompous attitude; inflated opinion of self.)

MIDDLE FINGER

Normally the longest on the hand, it indicates the part of oneself known as the superego. Its realm is the deepest level of consciousness. It is also the conscience.

General Length

Long. Good at organization, everything in its place; the perfect boss; studious, moody at times; love of education for its own sake; never stops the process of learning; loves puzzle-solving, perhaps an amateur Sherlock Holmes; may find such satisfaction in knowledge that forgets to participate in life and living.

Short—Almost Level with Index. May indicate a disorderly mind; carelessness with possessions; a bit sloppy; mind is always elsewhere; lacks positivity; moody or melancholy and unsatisfied; pessimistic or depression-prone; may feel "alone" in a crowded room.

Top Section. ORGANIZATION, IDEAS AND CONCEPTS, SUCCESSFUL, CURIOUS

Long. This single fingertip, if long, can bring up the entire aspect of a hand from failure to success; well organized; desires to know *some*thing about *every*thing; curiosity; has capability; multitalented; a "bug" on self-education; intellectually honest; finds it difficult to touch others—or to say "I love you"; an investigative mind; love of mystery; interest in the normal and the unusual; a philosopher; retentive mind.

Medium. Practical; fairly well-organized; bright and interested in everything; happy within and content with his or her own company; not inclined to dishonesty; frank-speaking; does not tolerate fools well; never smug or too satisfied with self; always seeking improvement.

Short. May lack curiosity, drive, and desire for education; lack of ability to deal with abstract ideas and concepts; a bean-counter; remembers and quotes statistics.

(*Very* short. A warped outlook on life; may suffer from fears or imagined threats.)

Middle Section. GENEROSITY, EMOTIONAL BALANCE, TRUST, TOLERANCE

Long. This indicates a person who has a strong need for stability; desire for love and affection; home-loving; desire to serve or to help others; the "giver"; trusting; may read or write poetry; possesses a lot of tolerance; reacts to outside stimulus acutely; "motherly" if female, "nurturing" if male; feels need to be with and around others; creative home decorator and designer; loves color, especially shades of blue and green; loves mystery novels.

Medium. Warm; friendly; sympathetic; always reaching for romantic settings and love; idealistic; usually happy if love is being given; pride in making a good appearance; creative dresser.

Short. May indicate moodiness, inclined to negative thinking about self; takes on guilt even if it doesn't reflect on own acts; may have lack of motivation in love; slow to share; instinctively suspicious at first; can become very withdrawn and self-centered if unable to find love or be loved by someone else. A short section here indicates that one *needs* love to survive, and will seek it until it is found. This may occur later in life than for most people. The negatives in this short finger section may be erased if one is fortunate enough to find real love from parents, associates, or a mate early in life.

Lower Section. SELF-CONTROL, BUILDING, STABLE, RELIABLE, STRENGTH

Long. Stick-to-itiveness; determination; self-awareness; passionate desires and cravings; ambition to build and maintain a home; usually good at real estate; a strong feeling for land and property; need for a place to withdraw and be secluded; caution; strong morals; love of children and small animals; studious; stable and reliable; stubborn at times.

Medium. Will possess a strong stubborn streak with some flexibility; listens to reason; somewhat possessive; collects things, whether valuable or not; desire to own land and property; has to have a "special" place; footloose and feckless; always going off to be alone; may be undependable or undisciplined.

Short. Fickle; may have a short attention span; a distaste for the outdoors; possible instability of personality.

RING FINGER

This finger represents the persona or "face" shown to the world. Its realm is the ideals and aspirations of the inner self, as well as the interrelations with people encountered.

General Length

Long. Good relationships with people and their problems; a good listener; idealistic and sensitive; may have great technical skill or ability; always involved with projects of many types and descriptions.

Short. A realist; not generally an outgoing personality; unwilling to take a risk; prefers routine to adventure; may shy away from people; great at working for charities or benefits.

(*Very* short. May be afraid of life; introverted.)

Top Section. INTUITIVE, LOVE OF UNUSUAL, IDEALISTIC, EXPLORING

Long. Love of mystery and the unusual; usually concerned with helping humanity or on a more personal level helping friends; possesses taste, perception and an eye for form and color; technical interests; a natural teacher; generous; helpful.

Medium. Loves romantic settings; good interior decorating skills; idealistic; friendly; willing to offer help wherever needed; often loves to dance.

Short. Impractical; afraid of new situations and unsure of strangers; needs time alone; drawn to water in lakes, rivers, or oceans; conformist tendencies; may be stubborn or overbearing or pushy; works well at jobs which don't involve creative output or abstract concepts.

(*Very* long. The nonconformist who cannot live under anyone's rules; disinterest in personal appearance.)

Middle Section. GENEROUS, ROMANTIC, FRIENDLY, TENDER, RESPONSIVE

Long. Love of beauty; generosity of nature; a talent for mimicry; romantic; spontaneous; loves life and other people; sensitive; softhearted; good fashion sense; love for small animals, plants, and flowers; idealistic; perceptive.

Medium. Carries out projects well; creative and artistic; outgoing; spontaneous; warm and loving; stable disposition; loves fun and laughter.

Short. Unresponsive; lacks ideals or goals; fears to trust others; prefers to do things for self; hates to be patronized or "put down"; prone to sudden mood changes.

Lower Section. HARMONY, BALANCE, STYLE, POISE, MUSIC, ART, GOOD LISTENER, FRIENDSHIP

Long. Love of harmony and balance; outwardly oriented; has good sense of style; likes colorful or beautiful clothing; has a taste for light and airy atmospheres; enjoys music, gaiety, and parties; enjoys talking and entertaining; may have acute sense of hearing; artistic; creative.

Medium. Warm; generous; meets new people easily; has a love of pastels and jewels; likes nightlife and fun; good sense of humor.

Short. Prefers small groups and good conversation to loud groups; may have trouble making new friends; keeps thoughts to self; introspective; uses music to create moods or relieve stress.

(*Very* short. Maybe a gossip, perhaps malicious at times; practical joker; enjoys pratfall humor; refuses to face reality and lives in a dream world.)

LITTLE FINGER

This finger represents the deepest innermost urges. It relates to the ability to communicate, to analyze one's self and needs, and to achieve sexual harmony and fulfillment.

It represents the id, which is the deepest portion of the human mind.

This finger will naturally be shorter than the other three, and must be measured carefully. If it is more than one inch shorter than the finger next to it, it will be considered a short finger.

General Length
Long. Good ability to interact and communicate thoughts and desires; a need to share; an understanding of self; a special talent for working with ideas; love of mystery and the unexplained.

Short. Inability to communicate well; shyness; hesitancy; a vulnerability of nature; preference for the tried-and-true rather than the new and strange; may have problems in romance relationships; unable to give.

Top Section. COMMUNICATIVE, HONEST, VARIED INTERESTS, WIT
Long. Good mental abilities; quick wit; love of communication by all methods; honesty; writing ability; some inability to make up the mind and stick to decisions; a good teacher; attention span may be a bit short; fantastic at creative ideas and abstract thought. (If very long tip, it is known as the "telephone finger," as it is usually found punching up someone to talk to.)

Medium. Needs communication with one special person; makes friends well; trusting; loves and needs to share; good at doing almost any job that involves communication ability.

Short. May be unable to communicate easily; afraid to trust others; slow to make good friends.

Middle Section. DISCRIMINATING, MATHEMATICAL ABILITY, SELF-ANALYSIS
Long. Intricate mentality; able to deal with complex prob-

lems; math and science natural to this personality; honest and understanding; versatile mind.

Medium. Can sustain interest over long periods of time; ability to learn quickly in-depth; retains information easily; discriminating; good business skills; ability to work with figures and statistics; enjoyment for the task at hand; good digestion, although a meager eater.

Short. Inability to grasp abstract concepts; dislike for or inability to work with figures; lacks taste.

(*Very* short. May be biased or prejudiced. When extremely short or even absent, it is one of the signifiers of hereditary mongolism.)

Lower Section. INTENSE, INVESTIGATIVE, MAGNETIC, CURIOUS

Long. Intensity of nature and emotions; a magnetic attraction for the opposite sex; love of mysteries and puzzles; the natural detective; curious about almost everything; loves to read murder mysteries; fearless; interest in psychic experimentation; a strong personality.

Medium. A strong need for love and tenderness; adventurous; interested; a quick mind; loves a secret and can keep one; hates surprises; a good planner.

Short. Lack of concern for the emotions or well-being of others; may be selfish; possible inability to achieve satisfaction in sexual matters; impatient; may have a morbid fear of death and dark places; moody.

(*Very* short. Can be a physically violent person with explosive temper and reactions.)

The sections of the fingers can give a complete analysis of the basic personality if measured and analyzed. The information gained is even more varied and interesting than that revealed by the skin patterns. It is important to measure

from the joints very carefully, so that an exact measurement
may be gained.

FAT-FINGERED COOKS AND HOUSEWORK HATERS

One unusual factor which is common to many hands is
an enlargement from side to side rather than from top to
bottom of the finger sections. It is most often found on the
index finger.

If the finger section is puffed up, bulgy, and enlarged,
the person may be a natural chef, able to create delicious
foods and baked goods at the drop of a hat—but will,
however, hate to do housework.

5

LINES AND SIGNS

In the past, the deep lines or channels on the hand have been the stock-in-trade of the palmist or fortune-teller. Almost everyone knows they have a lifeline, and if they notice it at all, they look at the length to see if it is short or long.

In modern hand analysis, the length of the line is not acknowledged to predict longevity. What it does record is the *vitality* of the individual.

Lifelines may either circle the thumb, beginning above the point where the thumb begins, running down toward the wrist, or may in some cases stop short or swerve over into a line running up the center of the hand. All of these positions have meanings, none of them bad news for the person.

The majority of lifelines will follow the rounded curve of the fleshy mound beside the thumb. (*See Major Lines handprint.*)

This is a normal position for the lifeline, and whether it

Major Lines

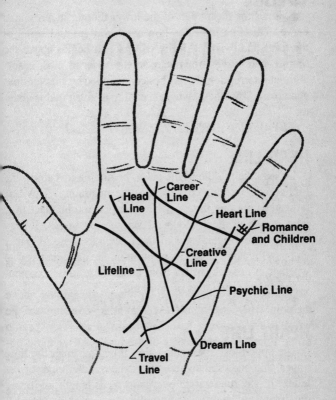

Head Line

Career Line

Heart Line

Romance and Children

Creative Line

Lifeline

Psychic Line

Dream Line

Travel Line

is long or short should be of no concern, for the *appearance* of this line is of much more importance than its length.

THE MAJOR LINES

LIFELINE

Follows the fleshy part of the lower thumb, in a rounded curve. This line indicates how vital you are and some of the turns and twists each life will take. It begins above the thumb, and curves downward to the wrist in most cases, without interruption. It may be accompanied by smaller lines and crossed by others, whose meaning is given in this chapter.

KEY WORDS: VITALITY, ENERGY

HEAD LINE

Crosses the middle of the palm, beginning just above the lifeline or intermingled with it at the beginning. This line indicates how one thinks, what direction the intellect may take, and how much independence one possesses. It may be crossed by several sets of lines, such as those of career and psychic ability, and its position on the hand may reveal whether or not one suffers from headaches, stress, tension, or breathing difficulties of any kind.

KEY WORDS: THOUGHT, INTELLECT

HEART LINE

The uppermost line in the palm, it begins under the little finger, and ends somewhere under the middle finger or the index. It may run straight over most of its length, or it may dip downward slightly, and usually ends in a short "brush" or forked set of lines. This line indicates the general health and circulatory system, including heart and blood chemistry, capacity for sympathy or empathy, and ability to care about

others. Everything that affects one's state of health will leave
a mark on this line.

KEY WORDS: HEALTH, SYMPATHY

CAREER LINE

Runs upward from the base of the palm toward the fingertips. It is unusual to find one of these which has no interruptions along its length. When motivations change, or one changes a basic career direction, the line itself will move and change.

This line indicates whether one is doing something with one's life, and what efforts at achievement have been made. Its ending under one or another finger will show the type of career direction chosen, whether in business, the arts, politics and law, or medicine.

The career line may be crossed by a multitude of other lines, lying as it does in the center of the palm, and will sometimes be accompanied by a thinner "shadow" line, which indicates a career direction that is being abandoned in favor of a stronger, better one.

KEY WORDS: MOTIVATION, DIRECTION, APPLICATION

PSYCHIC LINE

This line begins low in the palm, either near the beginning of the career line, or, in some cases, starts deep in the fleshy pad at the outside of the lower palm, which is the realm of imagination.

It indicates ability to utilize the mental capacities of intuition and perception. Psychic is a word which refers to affairs of the mind as well as the more popular version involving ESP. This line can indicate strength of mind, capacity for utilizing one's sensitivity to those nearby, and potential for developing intuition and ESP.

KEY WORDS: INTUITION, SENSITIVITY

There are a number of less obvious but just as important lines whose meaning we will cover later in this chapter.

THE LIFELINE

One of the most important in the hand, it is never absent. Whether it is long or short is immaterial. What *is* of importance are lines which *cross* the lifeline, or lines that shoot off the lifeline upward toward the fingers, or downward toward the wrist.

OFFSHOOT LINES

UPWARD. If there are small, almost vertical lines of one-quarter inch in length that begin on the lifeline and point upward toward the fingers, these are periods of intense activity in the life of the owner, or times in which he is trying hard to improve the quality of his environment. This might be by going back to school or college to further education or to get a degree. In this case, the upright line may run from the lifeline upwards to the middle line of the hand, which is known as the head line. The touching of the one line to the other acts almost like an electrical cord, connecting the life circumstances to the intellect.

In some cases, the line may go all the way up to the uppermost line, known as the heart line. This would indicate that he has begun a career which involves something very close to his heart or something he has always wanted to do.

In rare cases, it may indicate that the owner has finally found the perfect mate he or she has spent a lifetime searching for.

DOWNWARD. Short lines which run at a downward angle from the lifeline may indicate either periods of depression, something unpleasant which disturbed the life, or periods of illness. The placement on the line at which any of these lines appears will indicate the age at which they occurred, or will occur.

DATING ON THE LIFELINE

The lifeline begins above the thumb. Often it begins exactly at the place where the skin of the hand becomes the lined skin of the palm. You will have to bend the thumb down to make certain. Each inch of the line covers approximately twenty years in time and events can thus be dated correctly by dividing each inch up into twenty sections. It is possible to be very correct in this time placement if you will take the time to measure the length of the lifeline.

CHAINS

In the early portion of the line, it is common to find what looks like a small chain between the heart line and lifeline rather than two distinct lines. This is due to the spate of childhood diseases we all suffer under the age of ten or twelve. In the hands of people twenty-five and under, it will be less significant, because of the many types of vaccines which are now given to young children. In older persons, the chaining may be significantly involved over the first half-inch of the line, indicating illnesses.

Chains lower on the line will indicate similar problems, although not involving diseases of childhood such as measles or mumps.

UNUSUAL ENDINGS

The lifeline, as I have stated, may deviate from the normal curve, and branch out into the middle of the hand, where it usually flows into the Career line which runs vertically in the center of the palm. This is usually regarded as a strengthening of the line which is otherwise short, as the merging with the Career line indicates a person who both has and enjoys his purpose in life (career).

A lifeline which ends in a sort of brush or many-branched formation indicates that there will be complications of some type at the end of the life, whether of health or circumstances. This should not be taken as unavoidable, however, as all of the lines on the hand can and do move and change when you yourself change and grow as a person.

SHORT LINES

As I've said before, a short lifeline does not indicate a short life. This fallacy has been disproven by examining the hands of persons after death. Several studies have been done and information gained that many persons with overlong lifelines died at a young age, and conversely, persons with short lines lived very long lives. An individual whom I know personally, and who has a very short lifeline, is now in her late seventies and shows no sign of an "early" death.

CROSSES AND TRIANGLES

In some hands, there is a small "x" or cross that lies close to the lifeline, which is touched only by one arm of the x. This is known as the "lifesaver's" cross, and it indicates that at some time during your life you will help save the life of another human. Owners of these lines have reported incidents of pulling a drowning swimmer out of the water; giving the Heimlich maneuver to a choking child in a restaurant; and a great variety of interventions to avert what could have been fatal incidents. It is considered a sort of blessing to find this cross on the lifeline, as it is not given to us all to help or to actually save a life.

It is sometimes found on the hands of doctors and nurses, on whose hands it would be expected. In fact, it is quite rare on these hands.

Tiny triangular formations may appear on the lifeline, and if so, are often indications that a surgical operation has been performed. The age of the individual at that time can be accurately determined by measuring the lifeline and dividing it.

A tiny triangle near the beginning of the lifeline on hands of older persons may indicate that they had poliomyelitis (polio) as a child if there is a microscopic cross within the triangle; or if there is a dot within it, the person will have suffered scarlet fever or one of the more serious diseases of childhood.

THE TRAVEL LINE OR "WILD GOOSE SYNDROME"

On some hands, there is a distinct branching off from the lifeline near the bottom of the line, and extending out toward the career line but not touching it.

This is the mark of the person who loves to travel, whose home is where he hangs his hat, or who is required to travel constantly because of his job. This line does not appear on the hand in early childhood, but appears later.

Splits, lines which run parallel to the lifeline, or islands, where the line actually splits and separates, forming a sharp-ended oval, will indicate periods of uncertainty, confusion, distress, pressure, and even disease.

If a lifeline is islanded like that, one is probably under too much pressure and should clean the irritants out of one's life as rapidly as possible.

ENDINGS

In my files are a wide variety of lifeline endings, from ones which cross the hand and join with the Career line, to those which actually move over and begin again somewhere

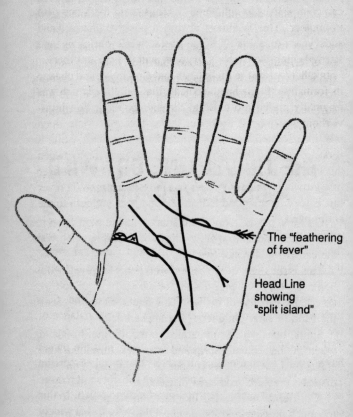

The "feathering
of fever"

Head Line
showing
"split island"

**Common Line Formations
(See Chapter 7: Your Hand and Your Health)**

along the length of the line. This is the clearest indication possible that the human mind, determination, and willpower can control lives to completely change them from one path to another. This is almost always a positive change, and adds years to a life in some cases; while enriching and strengthening the owner's maturity and growth in others.

In other words, the lifeline can and does move and change its formation. Some hands indicate that a lifeline which was originally placed too close to the thumb, indicating introversion, has moved itself out into a better or more open position. Sometimes a print will show this process while it is occurring, and there will be a small "trace" line between the old line no longer being used, and the new, stronger line growing beside it further out into the palm. Wherever this is seen, it is a good indication, and adds strength to the entire hand.

This was called a "sister" line by palmists, and was thought to be a sign of protection. In some ways, that thinking may be not totally incorrect, for when the line has been moved, it is always for a positive result.

If this double line is seen along with a travel line, then the owner may move to another country for the balance of the lifetime.

If the travel indication appears by itself, and the owner has not done much traveling, it may be that he takes "dream voyages" because his job or position in life does not require him to travel, or that he has no opportunity to do so. In this case, it will represent a subconscious desire to travel widely which continues throughout the life span. In the hands of older adults, this may be fulfilled by their going on cruises or foreign trips much later in life than would be expected.

BEGINNINGS

There are only a few important things to look for at the beginning of the lifeline.

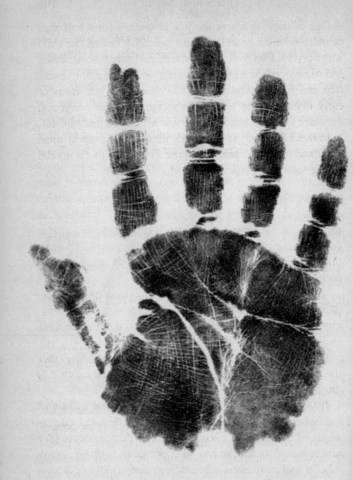

The Lifeline

Life and Head Line twined first twenty years of life.
Note confused Career Line. Blurs on Head Line
indicate headaches. Frustration Lines on thumb very
apparent—owner feels constricted by life.

One of these is where the line is merged for a half inch or more with the head line. The indication is that the child was very closely held within the family circle, had strong and often overbearing parents, and thus was unable to break free and form his own personality until the late teens or early twenties. The longer the merged portion continues, the older the child was when he was set free to find himself.

In rare cases, this is caused by illness, and even in some rare examples, the child was quite ill or perhaps an invalid during the early portion of the life.

INDEPENDENCE. If the lifeline begins completely separated and alone and does not attach itself to the heart line, the childhood would be one of more independence, perhaps too much so. At some point in the first fifteen years there will have been a period of rebellion from parental control. This develops a much stronger personality; whether for better or worse may be determined from the rest of the hand.

EXTREMELY HIGH. In some cases, the lifeline will begin very high on the palm, less than an inch below the index finger. This is a sign of a powerful and charismatic personality, a natural leader, teacher, and perhaps a mastermind. *(See figure, p. 4)*

This position is rare, but is encountered on some hands. If it is present, the lifeline should be given extra consideration, and other signs of this strength of personality should be sought in fingerprints and finger lengths. It would be expected that the index finger would be much longer than the ring finger when found with this lifeline beginning.

If, however, this line position is accompanied by an index which is much shorter than the ring finger, you will find a personality which is completely frustrated; as the leadership natural to this high beginning will have encountered a self-image problem and thus turned inward, frustrating the owner.

This would be extremely rare.

VITAL SIGNS

If the lifeline is strongly curved out into the palm, with a rounded curve as it drops lower, the person's vitality and energy are naturally strong. This is a doer, not a dreamer. The further the curve is drawn out, the more the potential for strength of personality and mind will be. Strength in this connection does not refer to muscle, but mentality.

If the lifeline is barely curved along its length, the individual's strength will be less. There may be good motivation at the beginning, but plans are not carried through completely. This type line may also signify the person whose energy potential is insufficient. He is not lazy, but does not have the strength required to follow things through.

If the lifeline is almost straight, running close to the thumb along its length, then the personality may be introverted, even fearful of failure, and thus may prefer the tried-and-true rather than to take the initiative.

Given the right stimulus, the lifeline can be moved out into the palm and the personality strengthened. In some cases, this will result in an intersection with the Career line, and the strengthening will take place because of and in conjunction with the career. This adds impetus to anything the owner has chosen to do, and is always a sign of the successful person.

You may give this interpretation to any hand whose lifeline touches the career line at any point along its length.

If the lifeline crosses the entire palm and ends up on the lower outside pad, the possibility is that the personality is one which has no direction, and is fond of change and variety in the environment. Such people may be jet-setters who travel widely, but for no purpose other than enjoyment.

They hate to put down roots anywhere, and may leave family and home to wander for most of their lives. An unusual and interesting position.

The lifeline is a provocative one, but since the entire line is subject to movement and changes in position, length and aspect, it is wise to place less stress on this line than would be placed on the other three major lines in your hand.

It is acceptable to point out past events, present directions, and any current trends and directional signals you see, but be warned that the future may find the lifeline moving in one direction or another, even merging with the Career line at some point, which would give it an entirely new interpretation.

Remember, the hand is like a tape recorder. It can reveal the past and the present; it can indicate motivations and trends; but it is unwise to predict events far into the future.

THE HEAD LINE

This line is also subject to change, and may have so many different formations it would take an entire chapter just to list each of them. To keep things simple, there are several formations of more importance than others, and we will cover these in detail.

The line that crosses the middle of the hand reflects the capacity to use one's mind, creativity, and anything going on within the brain itself. It can indicate ability to express oneself, especially in writing, and may predict a career in some form of writing from journalism to poetry, to historical fiction or biography.

A strong head line can strengthen the entire hand. If fairly straight, the person is a linear thinker, logical and perceptive. If curved, thinking is a bit more affected by emotions about things, and the input of imagination will be stronger.

Drooping deeply into the hand, even past the Psychic line and on into the pad of imagination, it could indicate an inventor or creator of new ideas and objects. This individual could also be so involved with a life of imagination as to prefer it to the harsher realities.

Most head lines do not cross into this position of the hand, but run diagonally across the palm, ending about an inch from the outside edge of the hand.

BEGINNINGS

If the head line beginning is entwined with the lifeline, then the childhood will have been a normal one of learning and growing under the guidance of the parents and other authority figures. In this case, the mature personality is slower to emerge, and the point where the separation begins will tell the age at which you began to be your own person.

If the head line begins just above the lifeline, then you have a strong streak of independence within you; the farther above the lifeline, the more this quality intensifies. (See figure, p. 4) If there is a half-inch separation, the personality can be considered "as independent as a hog on ice," in the old saying; for you will follow no one else's rules comfortably. People with this separated head line will fight for their independence, and usually will achieve it. They make better bosses than employees. If unable to reach the status of boss, they should work toward someday owning their own business.

If you have this widely separated head and lifeline, you will always feel that better things await you, and will work tirelessly toward becoming truly independent.

If the head line begins high up on the hand on the pad or bump of flesh below the index finger, the owner is a genius. The talent may be for improvisation, invention, research, or finding new ways and meanings in old ideas.

This position also indicates a restless mind, always looking for new information and new problems to solve.

A head line beginning closely under the index finger denotes a quick mind, lightninglike understanding, diplomacy, and the ability to convince *anyone* of *anything*.

MARKS

As the line sweeps across the hand, it may swing upward toward the heart line, in which case emotion may overpower your ability to be objective, at least during the years in which this deviation occurs. As the head line is dated exactly as the lifeline is, it will be easy to discover when this occurred, and how long it continued. Each half inch of the head line covers fifteen years in approximation. It is usually not as long a line as is the lifeline, so timing is slightly more difficult, but not impossible.

If the line dips toward the lifeline, there are remnants of early life embedded in the mind. One may have undergone traumatic events in childhood or adolescence. If so, the dip toward the lifeline, indicates that these events left permanent scars on the personality. Many of us do not realize how powerful these subconscious memories are, even though outwardly we are unable to remember them. So if the line dips in this manner, one may have had a harsh or unhappy youth, but overcome it and put it behind one, at least consciously.

"MYSTIC" CROSS

This is a large "x" formation which connects head line and heart line. In the old days it was considered a mark of psychic ability. What it actually means is that the person has achieved the merging of mind and emotions, so as to be an extremely well-balanced and perceptive individual. If one has this x, it will not signify any mystic ability, but it

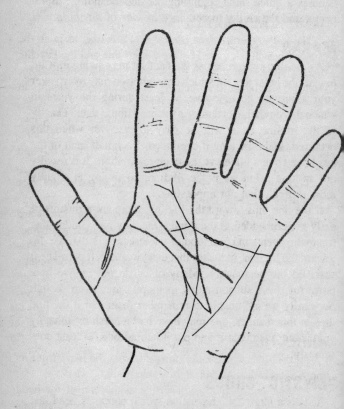

Mystic Cross

Note Lifeline "splice" into Career Line.
Note chaining of Heart Line could indicate eye
problems. See Chapter 7.

will indicate a pretty good grasp on both sides of one's makeup, and that head and heart are working together very well.

OTHER MARKINGS

Naturally, there are interruptions in this line, as in all the major lines. It is crossed by the Career line and the Psychic line. There are sometimes tiny chained portions of this line, and these indicate too much stress and that one should cut down on the workload for a while.

Small dots along this line indicate headaches, or the tendency. Susceptibility to migraine is indicated by larger dots, which might have open centers if you look at them through a magnifying glass.

Tiny crossing lines may indicate a lack of potassium. See Chapter 7 for more information.

Fine, hair-thin lines which whip upward or downward from the head line indicate periods of confusion or distraction. Again, the time periods may be determined by measuring off the line in half-inch, then quarter-inch segments ($\frac{1}{2}$" = 15 years, $\frac{1}{4}$" = 7 years). You can come to within a certain year's length by pinpointing these periods of overstress if you measure carefully.

DIRECTIONS

A head line which ends straight across the hand from its beginning indicates a straight thinker.

A thin, one-inch subsidiary line at the end of the head line is called a hanging head line. It may indicate periods of inability to think straight or to handle stress, and possible depression. When treatment is sought and the problems conquered, you will find this subsidiary line rejoins the head line.

A head line that drops deep into the hand indicates a

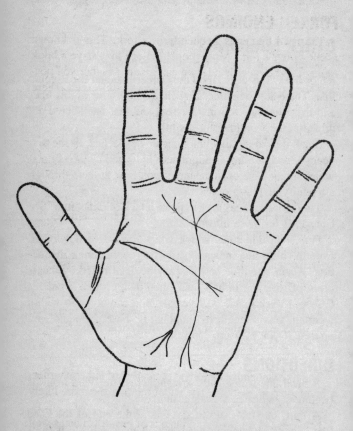

Forked Endings

possible depressive tendency, or an overactive imagination, if it ends low on the outer pad of the palm.

FORKED ENDINGS

The head line ends frequently in a fork. This is known as the writer's fork. Most people believe they have a book in them. From your hand, you can assess whether you possess the talent, and in what area you would excel. These are:

1. Forked at outside edge of hand, almost straight across from head line beginning — journalism or reporting facts

2. Forked downward, ending below the line of the beginning of the thumb — nonfiction, biographies, articles, features

3. Forked low in the hand in a diagonal line toward outside lower palm — fiction, romance, suspense, mystery

4. Forked very low, onto thick pad at the bottom outside edge of palm — romantic fiction, historical fiction, poetry

The line that ends in a fork is indicative of either a writer, a humanitarian, or both. The wider the fork the more likely the individual is to actually try writing.

I have found this ending on hands of businessmen as well as construction laborers, all of whom confessed their early adventures in the field of writing. In many of these hands, the fork was very narrow, signifying that they would not carry through this type of career.

If the forked ending is combined with a long tip on the

little finger, then the writing talent may be put to use in speaking in public. Although these people do not write articles or books, they can and do inspire others through speeches and lectures, or they may become expert story-tellers using voice and gesture to spellbinding effect.

EXTREMELY LONG OR SHORT HEAD LINES

A head line can be considered short when it does not extend past the middle finger. A long one may reach to the other side of the hand.

Although not an indication of the intellect or mental power, these long or short head lines merely represent the attention span of the individual. Very short lines indicate an attention span that lasts long enough to get the meat out of the book or idea being studied. These people often take speed-reading courses to enhance thi. quick comprehension. They are usually involved in several dozen projects at once. It could be called the Executive Head Line.

An overlong head line indicates that a person's power of concentration is stronger and slower, and they'd prefer to do one thing at a time and do it well. If a person with a long head line encounters too much pressure and too many things to do all at once, then the line will be marked with the small "cuts" of pressure, or the dots of headaches, etc. Migraine often shows by an almost perfect small triangular form on the head line, and is found more often on the long head line.

BREAKS IN HEAD LINES

Small islands can appear on the head line, where the line actually splits apart for a short distance. *(See figure, p. 106)* This can indicate some malfunction of the brain. See Chapter 7 for more on this.

An actual *break* in the head line may represent a diametric change in the line of thinking rather than a nervous breakdown. Some of the hands on which it is found belong to persons who have changed their religion, completely changed their profession (check career line, too) or drastically changed their way of life at the time indicated by the break.

Often, there is a trace line dropping down from the middle finger to this point, and in this case, it represents intellectual achievement of the highest type. The person may have written a book, done something spectacular, and, either way, his life will be completely changed from what it was, to another track. This is also found in the hands of winners of giant lotteries, whose lives have certainly been transformed.

A trace line from Career may represent the end of a bad partnership or even marriage, and the beginning of a new life.

If there is a stressed, chained line from the thumb area, then it is probable that the change is the result of the removal of some repressive family influence from the life—a visible "cutting of the apron strings."

Breaks are uncommon, however, and when they appear on the hand, should be given due attention, as the head line itself could be considered the most important line on the hand.

After all, the way the brain operates, and the strength and influence of the mind upon one's actions should be given utmost consideration in any analysis of the hand.

THE HEART LINE

Heart lines begin on the outside of the hand under the little finger, no matter what you may have read previously. When I began my study of the hand, I believed it to begin on the mound beneath the index or middle finger, and made many unfortunate mistakes in events.

In 1965, I discovered that the line actually begins unde the little finger, which changed the whole thrust of hand analysis.

In Chapter 7, you will also find that the small island formations under the ring and little fingers pertain to the eyesight and even to the teeth, indicating problems with these physical areas.

MEANINGS

The heart line has nothing to do with whether you love or are loved. It indicates the health of the circulatory system the heart itself; some physical malfunctions that react upon the blood or blood chemistry; and in some cases, the emotional capacity of the owner.

It also represents some of your energy potential and vitality, as does the lifeline.

If it runs low in the hand, quite close to the head line then you may have trouble separating your emotions from your logic.

A small area which seems to twist even closer to the head line indicates a portion of life in which both emotions and thought were under stress, usually because of a very difficult period.

If there is a visible "white-out" on this line, where the line refuses to print, or a deep depression is seen on the hand, the indication is that your feelings about yourself may be suffering from some stress or pressure coming from without. A repressive father or mother, a domineering spouse a demanding and abusive boss may be the cause. Its appearance on the hand indicates that one is being victimized by someone, and the situation is out of control.

My advice in this case would be to seek some competent counseling to avert further damage to one's self-respect.

A heart line that runs very high in the hand, just below

he fingers, would indicate a person whose emotions are
ightly controlled. The very high-set line is rarely seen.

MARKINGS

Some of the common markings will be given in Chapter
7, as they have to do with the blood chemistry, the eyesight,
and the teeth.

Chaining is often seen at the beginning of the line, which
will indicate childhood diseases, as does the lifeline in the
same place. Periods of high fever are indicated by sharp
diagonal lines shooting off the line at an angle. *(See figure,
p. 106)*

A completely chained line would indicate systemic problems all through the life. A thin shadow line beneath the
heart line will indicate a heart murmur—not a double life.

ENDINGS

There are many possible places for the heart line to end.
If it sweeps across the hand in a strongly rounded curve and
ends on the pad beneath the index finger, it indicates a person
who is self-centered to some degree. This is not all bad,
for sometimes one needs to pay more attention to personal
needs. If it shoots upward almost *into* the finger, you may
have a person who will be found on a rock-star stage, or
in politics or acting. They will become public figures and
enjoy it richly.

If the line is very high and ends that way, the person may
be self-centered.

Heart lines ending between index and middle fingers indicate people who are more open, and the owners can participate in the giving and receiving of love and affection in
a normal manner.

Heart lines that curve strongly down into the hand and
then almost take a right-angle upward to the middle finger

belong to very special people. This formation is known as the Gift of Mercy and represents persons who are all heart. They have not only sympathy for others, but empathy to the point where they can feel another's pain. They usually refuse to judge others, but accept them on their own merits. If your hand has this formation you are likely to be beloved by those around you, and you will find that people are attracted to you strongly, for they feel good just talking to or being with you. If male, you will have many female friends who are just friends. If female, you may have a dozen male friends, on a purely platonic basis.

It is a very distinctive formation, and a valuable one to possess. On the hands of social workers, psychologists, school counselors and judges it is a positive asset.

Strong heart lines, which curve downwards into the hand belong to people who try to live by the Golden Rule and usually have a strong code of personal ethics.

The more closely to the bottom of the middle finger the heart line ends, the more insight into other human beings you will have—and with such understanding comes acceptance and not criticism.

An unusual heart line is one that drops down to touch or to cross the head and lifelines. This is a repressive type of line and the owner will be inhibited to some degree. It would be found by looking back into the life that there was a strong emotional trauma early in childhood; and this has molded the entire life into a form much different from what it would have been. This is also true of a heart line that has a branch line running down into the head and lifelines. In this case the parents may have divorced when the child was young, or one may have been an alcoholic or substance abuser. This trace line can also be caused by loss of a parent through death, abandonment, or other misfortune. It may also indicate sexual attack by some disturbed individual during the first ten to twelve years of life.

Trauma or horrifying events in early youth cause the splitting of this line, and if a person has it, some support group like Children of Alcoholic Parents or professional counseling may prove very effective in bringing this event out and countering its effects.

THE CAREER LINE

Traditional palmists called this line the fate line. What it actually represents is motivation and direction. It might be found on the hands of a person who never worked at any job, but nevertheless would spend all of their energies at doing whatever came to hand.

It is representative of individuality, and is found most strongly marked on the hands of dedicated individualists.

When this line is missing from the hand, it has been said that these people "make their own fate." This is only partially correct, as the owner tends to adopt the motivations of those around them, rather than follow personal inclinations. One who is content to follow rather than lead might have no career line on the hand.

It is also possible for the line to appear on the left hand only and not on the right. In this case, something has occurred that prevented the person from following his natural career. It could be a health difficulty, an accident that disabled the owner, or even some favorable event that prohibited further progress in career directions. A good example would be the hand of Grace Kelly, whose fine film career was terminated by her marriage and taking on the duties of a monarch in Monaco. Her strong career line was splintered at that point and only reappeared later when she took on the duties of a real ruler.

The career line can appear and disappear at different ages, and is measured from the bottom of the palm upwards. At the point where the line crosses the head line, the age is approximately 30, and the heart line marks the fiftieth year. So these most productive years from 30 to 50 are enclosed by both the major lines. The years from the teens to 30 seem to be the longest portion of the line, perhaps rightfully so, as they are the "learning" years when the personality and the abilities are formed and sharpened.

The career line is a very strong channel of energy, and its proximity to the lifeline makes it easily available to the lifeline to make a "splice" when the lifeline is weak. Any portion of this line that represents the past is available to the lifeline for use as a reinforcement. Thus, if the lifeline were weak and thin, a splicing line might form on the hand running into the career line. If this is seen, the bottom of the career line *becomes* the lifeline and takes on the same importance, while the broken-off lifeline may still be visible below the joining portion.

BEGINNINGS

The most common place for a career line to begin is at the base of the palm. It may run all the way up to one of the fingers from that point, or there may be portions that seem to be broken off, and the line begins again further up. These breaks indicate that career and motivation have changed and another direction taken.

Career lines may also begin on the lifeline an inch or so up into the palm. Probably the personality was slower in developing direction and impetus during the school years and only emerged in the late teens or early twenties.

If the line begins *inside* the lifeline and runs outward, the owner is almost a perfect reproduction of one of his parents and may possess little individuality of his own, until adulthood. If this portion of the line is chained and/or broken, look to see if the head line and heart line are also badly chained. If so, there was possibly a childhood spent under severe repression from parents or other authority figures.

If it begins normally, then runs into the lifeline, and further up emerges again, it may indicate a person whose natural personality development was stifled for a time by something not under his control. It could be that the individual was the oldest child in a large family, with many responsibilities, or that one or both of the parents were invalids or incapacitated. It is a giving up of one's own direction, if only temporarily.

Career lines that begin on the fleshy pad at the lower outside edge of the palm indicate that the person is subconsciously motivated almost all the time. If your line begins here, it indicates that you don't always realize just why you did a certain thing at a certain time of life, or why you changed your line of reasoning in midstream. This would be because of subconscious prompting.

Career lines beginning in this area often belong to inventive, creative, artistic people, extremely individualistic. If your career line begins here, it is probably true that you will make your own fate.

If the career line begins with a fork, you have a "foot in two worlds." You will be motivated in part by outside stimuli and events occurring around you and partially by the stirrings of the subconscious mind. You may always have two "careers"—one which is your job, and the other which is your pleasure.

MARKINGS

A block can appear on this line, which is a short, sharp line crossing just the career line and no other. This would be just what it looks like—a stopping point. One may have had to give up career for marriage and children, for instance. If the line begins again, higher up, the career does too.

A small line that goes upwards an inch or more might represent a hobby pursued at the same time that one is holding down a job.

If there is a right-angle line which springs off from the career line and then resumes going upward alone, it represents a change in the career from one job to another, yet still in the same industry. In other words, it could be that a fileclerk was promoted to a secretary, still within the same company or type of business. It is a step up, but the job will still be in the same field.

If the line splits up and another line begins above the split, then the career has changed, and the fileclerk has become an automobile mechanic, so to speak. Most career changes will not be quite that drastic, but the marking does represent a complete change in what you are doing.

ENDINGS

If the line continues straight upwards across the entire palm and into the area directly beneath the middle finger, then the career is in business and may lead to executive status.

If the line ends upon the pad below the index finger, then the career may be in law, politics, criminal justice, or some area that involves legality.

If it runs almost into the ring finger, the career will be creative and artistic, perhaps in publishing, fashion design, or architecture.

Rarely, it runs into the little finger. In this position, the individual will work with money, perhaps in banking, the stock market, or some similar job.

Your career line is one of the most important indications on the hand, as its impact on your life is often the difference between success or failure.

SECONDARY LINES

THE CREATIVE LINE

This line is a branch line which begins on the career line and usually runs directly up into the ring finger, or the pad beneath the finger.

The indication is that the life will be spent in one or another area of creativity, research, and discovery. It also indicates that the person has a fine artistic sense, and may actually *be* an artist.

In a few cases, it may run upwards into the pad below the little finger. In this position, it would indicate a person whose career is in some branch of science or medicine. If so, the indication is that the individual would be involved in research into rare diseases or some other aspect of discovery.

This line is very seldom seen and if it appears on your hand, you should pay serious attention to where it ends, for career aptitudes are shown clearly on the hand and should be taken into consideration when young.

Whenever it is seen, the owner has a questioning mind and a strong desire to discover the unknown.

THE DREAM LINE

This line enters the hand at the bottom outside edge of the hand, runs upwards for an inch or so, and stops.

It indicates that the owner dreams in color and usually remembers his dreams.

It is also an indication of a person who can find answers to problems while dreaming or daydreaming.

This is the mark of the subconscious mind emerging into the surface in its own way—through dreams. Along these lines, if you have this line on your hand you may from time to time dream future events before they happen. This is

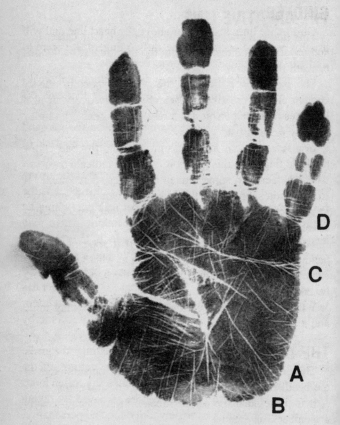

Unusual Line Positions

A-Creative beginning of career line
B-Dream lines
C-Career changes
D-Girdle under little finger

called "true dreaming" and often occurs with people who have this line.

GIRDLES

Girdles are lines that appear above the heart line and will usually be found encircling one or two fingers. It is rare to find one that encircles three or more fingers.

Palmists thought that girdles indicated emotional weakness, but this is incorrect. A girdle is a line that cuts off the strength of the finger beneath which it appears.

Cutting off the index finger would weaken the ego and self-esteem. It would thus create uncertainty and lack of conviction.

Under the middle finger, it would indicate that the strong superego is damaged, perhaps by outside influence; and the person is unable to achieve success because everything he plans seems to come apart, or ends in failure. There may be some feelings of guilt as well, even if they are not deserved. This is an unfortunate place to find a girdle, and can be overcome only by taking courses in motivation and self-confidence. It also may indicate that the personality has not been enriched by love, and is starving for affection. Fortunately, the effects of this girdle can be overcome by supplying what is needed.

Under ring and middle fingers at the same time, the girdle is often broken and chained in appearance, cutting off the owner from being effective in life. Perhaps shy, often humble and lacking force, this line can be removed by taking positive steps toward a more outwardly directed personality. Oddly, this is often found on the hands of actors, as it was on the hands of Montgomery Clift. It may explain why great actors so easily step into their part and almost *become* the person they are portraying, until the film, video, or play is over.

Not uncommon, but often found broken, this line should

be regarded as constricting the personality from growth and the forming of true individuality.

Under the ring finger alone, it indicates one who has trouble being creative and may have problems in drawing others to himself. It cuts off the attributes of the ring finger in the areas of interpersonal relationships, idealism, and friendship. Often, a person with this girdle has few friends and is very lonely, for he finds it hard to relate to others.

All of these things can be changed, of course, with the proper care and directional counseling.

Extremely rare, the girdle under the little finger has the effect of cutting the person off from his own personality. It also injures communications with others, as well as self-expression.

A girdle that enclosed middle, ring, and little fingers would indicate a person with severe problems in most of the areas of life and relation to the rest of humanity. Fortunately, most girdles of this type are found broken and split, thus indicating that the owner has made efforts to overcome this constriction of his personality.

If you have a girdle on your hand, it is likely that it will be split and broken. It could be interesting to note under which finger it is most broken, as that area indicates whichever portion of your personality was responsible for overcoming the strangling girdle. (*See figure, opposite page, for areas girdles would affect.*)

Girdles are not often found and are of great interest when evaluating a hand.

LOVE, AFFECTION, ROMANCE, AND CHILDREN

These areas of life are of supreme importance, and it is very easy to make a mistake in interpretation. It is necessary

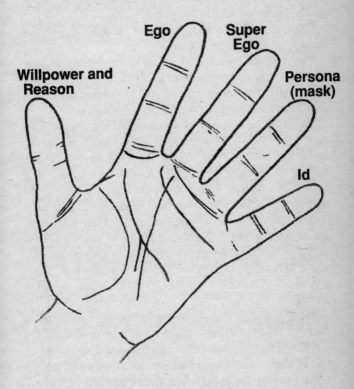

Ego   **Super Ego**

Willpower and Reason

Persona (mask)

Id

**Psychological Relationships
of Fingers**

to issue this caution before taking up this part of the palm for analysis.

Under the little finger, on the side of the hand, there are a number of horizontal lines. (*See figures, p. 99, 135*) They will be found above the heart line but below the finger itself. Often, they do not run far into the palm and may not show clearly except on the best of prints.

These are affection lines, and association lines, i.e., association with the opposite sex.

You may see one, two, three, or more of these lines. If the line is very close to the heart line, it would be considered in the early years of childhood, and probably represents a deep love for a parent, grandparent, or sibling.

As the space involved is so cramped, you should read the years of babyhood at the level of the heart line, and old age at the bottom of the finger. An early line would obviously be a parent or relative. As the lines appear in a higher area, perhaps ¼ inch above the heart line, they could indicate an early romance or two. Some hands will have two or three such early lines, indicating young romances. An association that lasted over a period of years will be a thin line and may droop downward as it comes onto the palm. This would indicate the end of the association. Some romances do not last long enough to merit this drooping ending.

Since marriage itself is only a human agreement and a piece of paper with or without a wedding ceremony, the hand cannot distinguish between romances, deep loves like that of Katharine Hepburn and Spencer Tracy which did not come to marriage, or actual legal marriages.

Do not feel that if you have three lines between heart line and finger you are doomed to have three marriages. What is actually indicated is either one romance and two marriages, or two romances and one marriage. It could even be three romances and *no* marriage.

If you see an unusually deep line, long enough to reach a half-inch into the hand, it is likely that this is a relationship of deep meaning, and long-lasting. It may actually indicate a marriage of the legal sort, or a twenty-year span of living and loving together.

To find the deepest and most meaningful of these lines, pull the tip of the little finger sideways away from the hand and see which of these lines becomes a deep channel. This is the most important of them all, and can represent the "perfect" marriage. If you find one of these lines, congratulate yourself, for it is a real blessing and rarely achieved.

All lines which droop downwards into the hand are ended associations. If the line actually drops down far enough to touch the heart line, it indicates the association was ended by divorce or by death.

If you were married to one person for ten, twenty, or more years, you will carry that mark forever, on your hand and in your heart.

If there is a line above that, then there will be another romantic association.

Judging the space is easy and makes the time factor understandable. Simply measure the space between heart line and the base of the little finger. Now divide it in two. This will be the 30th year, or if the space is more than a half inch in entire length, it might be the 35th year. Lines before that middle point would be prior to age 30 or 35; after that they will be in later ages.

I have seen hands whose deepest and strongest romance lines did not enter the hand until after age 50. There might have been three or four lesser lines below that one, indicating lost romances or marriages. And yet, the indication is that the owner of the hand has something to look forward to—the best is yet to come. Many men and women make early marriages and romantic mistakes, and yet when they've almost given up all hope, the right person enters their lives almost magically—and the heart is filled at last. If you have your deepest line well above that mid-mark, you will achieve that greatest of all human goals, a successful, loving, and giving marriage. Believe me, the heart is never too old to love. I've seen this mark on the hands of women in their fifties and sixties and watched with happiness as they found happiness and love at last. So it is possible and, if this mark is visible, inevitable. The only thing that could keep this from happening would be for you to turn your back on love, which is not likely.

CHILDREN

This is always an interesting line (or lines). The indications for children are in the same area as you find love and romance, not unnaturally.

These markings are vertical, while the romance lines are horizontal. You will need a clear print or a strong magnifying glass to see them.

The tiny vertical lines indicate your body's capacity to have children. It may be that you might decide not to have more than two children. If your hand indicates five of these marks, this is your own decision. The lines merely indicate that you *could* have that many children.

At times, you may find one child line on an association line, and perhaps one or two more on another association line above it. This indication is that the children were born of different fathers or mothers. A line which is short but crosses and appears on both sides of the association line is a live, healthy child. Straight up and down is usually a boy, tilted a bit is a girl.

If the line does not *cross* the association line, then the baby or child may be adopted, or a stepchild. A line on an early association line which does not cross it completely could indicate a miscarriage. Any child line that does not completely cross *any* association line indicates a miscarriage or abortion, whether spontaneous or induced.

It is rare, but sometimes a child line will be found which is split like a very thin oval. This would indicate a child born with a handicap.

A double line *very* close together and on one association

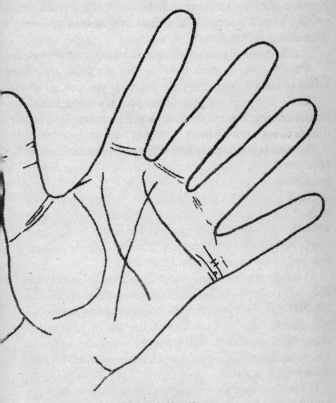

"Association"
or
Romance Lines and Children Lines

line might indicate twins. I've seen this several times, and it is usually true.

Keep in mind that you may have many child lines. I have at least a dozen on my own hand and only had six. The extra lines indicate possible children that could have been born, but we felt that six was enough.

An adoptive parent will grow the line, and the hands of some teachers will have a multitude of lines, as they tend to "adopt" a special child from time to time and almost feel that it is their own.

It is absolutely necessary to use a strong magnifying glass when looking at these lines, as they are small and out of sight around under the little finger. If you can get a clear look, you may set a childless person's heart at ease by discovering one or more lines yet to come. Or you may gladden your own heart by finding one for yourself.

A most interesting, if small, area of the hand, indeed.

6

A COMPATIBILITY INDEX

HOW COMPARISON WORKS

Obviously, a male hand will be different from a female hand in its size. Male hands do tend to have fewer palmar lines than their female counterparts. And on these hands, the skin patterns are of perhaps even more importance than they are on female hands, as lines may be few.

Does this mean that a man has fewer complexities of personality than does a woman? Not necessarily.

Although it is true that often opposites attract, in the world of hand analysis, it is the *similarities* that reveal whether one person has a chance of compatibility with another. Those features that are similar in each hand thus offer more chance at true love and friendship, which are the basis of any romantic or marital relationship. Science tells us that no two fingerprints are ever like another; and the palmar skin patterns are just as distinctive. What has not yet been revealed is that each human hand possesses this same uniqueness in its shaping and the size of the finger sections as well. It is obvious, then, that no two sets of hands are going to be exactly alike in every area, any more than your right hand is exactly like your left.

If a handprint comparison could be done upon meeting another individual, there would be less stress in human relationships, not just in love and marriage. As this is not practical, we can examine the hands of another by sight alone, yielding us a fairly firm basis on which to make judgments. If you could watch and observe the hands of Johnny Carson or Vanna White every time you saw them, you could make some very accurate character assessments without ever seeing them in person. How much more accurate could you be, then, if you had the opportunity to see and observe a hand at close quarters.

YOUR COMPATIBILITY CHECKLIST

HAND SHAPES	COMPATIBILITY
Action (rounded hand, widespread fingers)	Action, Technical, Mental
Technical (squared-off palm, broad fingers)	Mental, Action, Emotional
Mental (long, rectangular palm, smooth, long fingers)	Technical, Emotional
Emotional (long, thin palm with slight knobbiness of knuckles on thin fingers)	Technical, Mental, Emotional

Least compatible: Action hand with Emotional hand. The fast-moving mind of Action does not blend well with the sensitive mind of the Emotional type.

FINGERTIPS	COMPATIBILITY
Squared off or blunted tips	Squared or softly rounded tips
Rounded tips	Squared or rounded tips
Sharply rounded tips, almost pointed	Blunted tips, almost square
Bulging tips, larger than other finger sections	Rounded tips

Least compatible: sharply rounded tips with blunted tips. The wit and sometimes insensitive outspokenness of the almost pointed tip does not mesh well with the easily angered, egocentric attitudes that go with the bulging tipped fingers. Both are quick to anger, and irritation would be a real problem.

FINGERNAILS	COMPATIBILITY
Rounded, oval nails	Square nails
Highly arched nails	Arched square nails
Flat, round nails	Flat round or square nails
Wedge-shaped triangular nails	Broad, flat nails, of squared shape
Overlong nails, usually rounded	Square nails

Least compatible: broad, flat, and squared-off nails with highly arched nails. The slower-to-act personality which is indicated by flat, square nails cannot compete with the quicksilver mind of the highly arched nail. Noncomprehension, anger, or even jealousy may be the result.

FINGERPRINTS	COMPATIBILITY
Arch print	Arch, Loop arch, looped
Looped print	Loops, Loop arch
Loop Arch print	All types
Double Loop print	Loop, Loop Arch
Peacock Feather Loop print	Arch, Loop

Least compatible: Double loop with arch, as the straight-thinking and logical arched print cannot deal with the complex thinking of the double loop personality.

THE PALM	COMPATIBILITY
Highly padded hands, with small bulges under each finger, moist	Highly padded, or gently padded hands
Flat hands, little padding, cool, hard-feeling skin	Softly padded hands with thin padding under fingers
Softly padded hands, warm and resilient to the touch	Highly padded hands
Flat hands with soft texture	Softly padded hands with warm, resilient skin

Least compatible: flat hands with cool or moist hard-textured skin and long fingers are least compatible with warm, resilient, highly or softly padded hands.

PALMAR LINES	COMPATIBILITY
Hands with career line	Hands with incomplete or splintered career line

Hands with incomplete career line	Hands with complete career line
Hands with no career line	Hands with complete career line, mid-palm
Hands with career line coming up out of imagination portion of palm	Hands with complete career line up middle of palm
Hands with career line independent of all other lines and mid-palm	Identical hands, or hands with career line coming from imagination area

Least compatible: Hands with no career line on either individual's palm. Also, hands with complete, independent career line running straight from wrist to bottom of middle finger possess such drive, motivation, ambition, and strength that they have problems relating to any person whose hand has no career line at all. A compatible relationship could only be formed if the individual without a career line was willing to give up his or her own individuality to follow the other person's dream. A hard life to endure.

NOTE: It should be remembered that palmer lines do move, change, and even appear on a hand after some major change in the life. If a person with no career line desires to change because of his association with another whose career line is clear and sharp, it is possible that a career line will begin at that age and continue upward from that point.

Psychic lines on the hand indicate that the person has some inborn sensitivity to those around him. This line upon the hand blends best with another hand which has the line, even if dim, hard to see, or vestigial. If both hands possess the psychic line, then a relationship of such closeness can be formed that the husband and wife may become almost like identical twins, in that they are attuned to each other in perfect harmony. At times, they can almost read each other's minds or may find themselves talking about a subject which is already in the mind of the other.

MOTIVATION

As discussed previously, each finger is divided into three sections. The bottom section, close to the hand, is the area wherein ideas are initiated.

The middle section of each finger is where ideas are "put together" and made more concrete.

The tip section of each finger is the area of actually bringing ideas to fruition.

The three sections of the fingers indicate your ability to initiate ideas, to reason them out and then to make them become real. This is an important part of compatibility, since if one member of a team possesses ideas in plenty, while the other is better at reasoning them out, then as a team they can achieve a great deal through their partnership. As the old saying goes, "you can't live on love"—in to-day's world it may be necessary for both partners to work, or if one works while the other stays home, then it is necessary for their goals to be the same. If one partner helps and supports the other by applying his inborn reasoning ability to the creative ideas of the other, then it is likely that they will not only have a successful marriage, but they will achieve financial security much more easily than a couple would whose motivational potentials do not match.

If, however, each partner has a different goal in life, then there may be problems in realization; or they may find themselves going in totally different directions. This would create a struggle for dominance, and only one could win.

It is a good idea, therefore, to carefully note the areas of life that the fingers themselves represent, and to check for the motivational and idea lines which run vertically upward through each section.

INDEX FINGER—	Career, self-esteem, ability to utilize one's abilities. Also education and leadership qualities.
Vocations:	Actor, politician, lawyer, business executive, astronomer, explorer, radio or television news, aerospace technology, drama or theater, cooking, chef
MIDDLE FINGER—	Business ability, generosity, the urge to self-educate, power, determination, and initiative
Vocations:	Real estate, insurance, business administrator or CEO, land developer, nonfiction writer, Wall Street investor, builder, banker, magazine or newspaper editor/writer
RING FINGER—	Creativity, idealism, love of people, ability to work with others, inventions
Vocations:	Psychologist, social worker, writer, travel agent, artist, medical researcher, architect, fashion designer, fiction writer, child care, paralegal, charity organizer, inventor, tinkerer, dressmaker or costumer, mechanic
LITTLE FINGER—	Communications, self-analysis, love of mystery, ability to project

	personality and maneuver others' minds
Vocations:	Advertising, accountant, stock market analyst, communications specialist, detective, radio or TV personality, systems analyst, medical professional (nurse, doctor, etc.), sales, promotion and publicity, paramedic
THUMB—	Willpower, intuition, logic and reasoning ability, sports ability
Vocations:	Professor, investigator, futurist, athletics expert or performer, religious leader, minister, etc.

In a child's hand, it is rare to find vertical lines on any finger, but there may be a few on the thumb, as it is the seat of willpower and some children make their personalities felt even while very young.

Even into adolescence and sometimes young adulthood, these lines may only appear on the lower phalange or finger sections. These represent ideas as most young persons may not yet know what they "want to be" in life, but ideas crowd their minds.

These lines generally begin to become visible on the middle finger sections in the mid to late twenties, and by age 30, they should have become numerous on one or more fingers, representing vocational areas.

VOCATIONAL COMPATIBILITY

It is obvious that the lines of motivation and achievement will appear on the upper fingertip sections only when goals are achieved. In marriage, it is possible for the two partners to have and achieve similar goals, or to work together for the *same* goal.

It is not unusual to find husband and wife happily working at totally different jobs or careers; yet if there is support for the desires and motivations of the other partner, a complete harmony of purpose can be achieved.

A marriage can unravel, however, if only one partner is growing and achieving, while the other is stagnating. Should this be the case, a thorough examination of the hand of the partner whose progress has stopped should be made; and he or she should be encouraged to return to school to complete the education lacking or to begin training for the job area in which the most numerous lines appear to be heading.

An Example. For instance, if the wife's bottom finger section on her index is the largest of the three sections, or if it is puffed out at the sides, it should be considered dominant. In this case, she might find satisfaction in some form of cooking or baking for others, perhaps as a caterer. As she is a born cook, this would supply her with a field in which to study, to learn, to grow, and perhaps to make some money of her own.

If the finger section is heavily lined, but not puffed out, then the talent may be for drama, and he or she should take some courses in theater and acting as a first step toward getting involved with amateur dramatics.

I have a friend, an astronomer, who prepares star-chamber presentations for adults and children at a planetarium and who acts in children's theater in the evenings. A conflict? Not for this person, who learned early that all talents should be explored and utilized.

Vocational compatibility is easily achieved when both marital partners take the time to support and motivate the other.

SEXUAL COMPATIBILITY

Psychological hand analysis can explore the depths of the human personality with accuracy, including the capacity to love and reach sexual fulfillment.

The most outstanding indication that sexual compatibility may not be possible is the very short lowest section on the little finger. This finger segment indicates the individual's capacity for love and desire for sexual completion, and if it is very short, or deeply crossed by horizontal lines, the person may have a lack of desire for love and physical expression or an inability to "let go" and participate.

The reasons for this may be hereditary, or may have been caused by some early trauma in the life. This indication often expresses itself by deep, horizontal lines, almost gashes, across the lowest segment of the little finger. As this finger signifies self-analysis, ability to communicate and the deeper urges within the human mind, these horizontal "blocking" lines may cut all of these areas off from free expression.

An event such as molestation, rape, incest, or another form of sexual trauma in childhood or adolescence might result in these deep blocks.

If the finger section is of normal length, crossed by few or no horizontal lines, then the potential for romance, love, and sexual fulfillment is good.

In comparing the finger sections, it is necessary to use a short ruler to make exact judgments, especially as there will be a size differential between male and female hands. If a finger section on a female hand is considered normal at 1 inch, and two sections are of that length, while a third is ¾ inch or less, that shortest segment must be given more attention, as it represents a repression in the area covered by that finger section. (See Chapter 4.)

If the finger sections are of equal length, but the lowest section is scored by deep horizontal lines, the effect would be the same as if the finger segment were very short.

MEASURING TIME

If the deep lines are very low and near the palm, then the traumatic event occurred very early in life. It may not be remembered by the conscious mind. It has left a scar, however, even if not remembered.

Should the line be within the first third of the finger section, it would be in later childhood or the teenage years.

If this type of blocking line appears in the middle third of the finger section, then it may be that the owner has had to deal with adult rape or a brutal husband.

These blocking lines are much less common on the little finger of a male, but there may be fainter, less distinct horizontal blocks in the section. This may represent some type of trauma, or an aspect of failure to perform as required. There will be a corresponding lack of self-confidence in matters of love and sexual compatibility.

Any couple whose hands show either the horizontal blocking lines, or a small, squeezed-down section at the bottom of the little finger should proceed slowly in matters of love. It would be of great help if they would seek premarital counseling. Many times, the events which caused the real problems are buried deep within the subconscious, and should be dealt with and dismissed. If this occurs, then the blocking lines will fade out and almost disappear to the naked eye. They will, however, continue to show up when an inked handprint is made.

Long Section at Base of Little Finger.
If the other finger sections are approximately ¾ inch in length and the bottom segment is 1 inch or more, then it would be considered to be long.

This long segment indicates those whose need for love, affection, and tenderness is one of the strongest drives in their lives.

The need for sexual completion will be equally strong, and because of this the problem may have surfaced early in adolescence. This indication would be shown by one or more horizontal blocking lines, but not of any great depth.

The longer the finger section, the stronger the sex drive, and the greater the potential for misuse in youth. It is also an indication that if matched with an individual who also possesses a long or overlong section on that finger, a highly passionate and fulfilling life will be the result.

The capacity for passion is not a negative thing, so long as it is channeled into a constructive outlet.

COMMUNICATION

The second factor in sexual compatibility involves the length of the *top* section of the little finger.

In some personalities, the need for someone with whom to communicate deeply is even stronger than the need for sex. A long tip on this finger is an asset to marriage or romance, as this need to communicate may be the keystone of a good marriage in which the partners share every aspect of their lives, and are good friends as well as husband and wife.

This might be considered the perfect marriage. If communication is easy, free, and consistently deep, other aspects of the marriage are easier to take and problems seem to iron themselves out without a wrinkle.

On a female hand, the section would be a bit longer than normal, perhaps 1 inch or more. The finger segment would appear to be long, even to the eye. (Adjust measurements for male hands.)

If this section is long or overlong on the hand of one partner in a romance while the section is short on the hand of the other, there will be little or no meaningful communication between the two.

The long tip on this finger is known as the mark of the good communicator, and while physical desire has limitations over the years, communication between minds has no limits.

If two persons with short tips on their little fingers meet, it is likely that there will be little or no communication between them, and even if passion or desire exists, it would be better to let things go no further. A one-faceted relationship has little or no staying power, once the physical attraction subsides.

Most Compatible. Hands which both possess either long tips and normal lower sections on little fingers, or long lower segments and normal tips, crossed by few or light blocking lines, would be very compatible.

A "perfect" hand would be one which has no imbalance in finger lengths, no blocks on finger sections, and some regularity in the line patterns, with a deep curve to both lifeline and heart line. This hand would signify almost completely normal function in the basic areas of life. The thumb would also be low set and spread somewhat from the fingers.

A close-set thumb, or a thumb which is set higher than usual, may indicate a person who has problems with self-expression, and may be unable to participate in the give-and-take of love. A very close-set thumb is also often suspicious of the motives of others, which may lead to unfortunate jealousy.

A high, tight heart line which ends on the base of the index finger may be an impedance to love and companionship, as the owner is likely to have little time for the needs of others, and could be considered cold and selfish because of this.

A low-set heart line with a sharp right angle up to the

base of the middle finger may be *too* forgiving and unde-manding in love matters, and so would be vulnerable unless his or her marital partner had the same heart line.

A long, overpowering index finger on the hands of one partner, with a short index on the hands of the other, would indicate the pants-wearing Archie Bunker and Edith type of marriage. In this situation, the partner with the short finger would never be allowed to experiment, to learn, or to grow.

Two hands with long, powerful index fingers would com-pete, and although this would be healthy in some cases, it may become a bit worrisome and wearing if the goals are different, and the partners are pulling in opposite directions.

If one person's hands have the dominant index finger, and the hands of the other are of normal length when com-pared with the ring finger, then a slight natural dominance is exerted and may add zest to the romance.

Ring Finger.

The middle section of this finger and the lower section at the base of the finger are important areas in which to consider romance or marriage.

If the middle section of the finger is the longest on that finger, then the owner will be an idealist, perhaps a dreamer, living much within himself or herself. Should a hand with this finger section measuring the longest encounter a person whose corresponding finger segment is quite short, there would be an almost impossible conflict. Short sections here are the mark of the realist, whose practicality would clash with the romantic idealism of the long-finger section. Like a butterfly, the beauty of the idealist would beat itself to battered ruin against the cold steel of the realist.

In choosing a life mate, it would be best if the middle sections of the ring fingers were of *equal* length—whether long or short.

The bottom section has to do with interpersonal relations, and a long segment here would indicate a person with many friends. It is also an indication of a person who likes to go out and about, to parties and gatherings of all kinds.

If the partner has a normal length lower section, this may not become a problem, as they could choose which events they would attend together and which would be fun for only one of the pair.

If, however, one has a long section and the other a very short lower segment, then there will be problems which may grow more severe over the course of the marriage; for the one with the long section will prefer parties and large groups of people, while the other partner with the shorter-segmented finger will prefer small groups, quiet times, and intimate discussions with a few friends.

The same may be true if one has heavy, deep horizontal lines crossing the lower section of the ring finger, for this may be an indication that he or she is of the retiring sort, preferring his or her own company. This type person will need quiet time and space in which to meditate and grow, which would inevitably conflict with the more gregarious partner.

Compatibility between man and woman is a thing to value, for in this age of easy divorce and three out of five marriages lasting only a few years, it would save many from a loveless existence, or the frustrated searching for the "right" companion or mate. It could also stop many mistakes *before* they happen.

7

YOUR HAND
AND YOUR HEALTH

Over the past twenty years, I have studied the hands of others for many reasons. One of the most important—and the most interesting—is the area of health, both psychological and physical.

Medical science is just beginning to catch up with the diagnostic possibilities offered by a computer and scanner, but it is interesting to report that in Europe, one of my observations concerning genetic defects as indicated by a marking on the hand has been proved to be correct. With their procedures and methods of computer checking, over seventy different DNA defects have been recognized and diagnosed. Some twenty years ago, I predicted that someday in the future, one would be able to step into a small cubicle, put both hands down on a scanner and get a complete read-out of physical health, good or bad. It seems now that this day may not be too far in the future.

Since the time of Aristotle, it has been known that the human hand was capable of indicating physical problems. Medical books usually contain a short chapter on the subject, and a dermatology text will contain a bit more. Some few physicians of today, like Dr. Milton Alter, have braved the ridicule of peer groups to announce important findings from the dermatoglyphic skin patterns of the hand. Dr. Alter's findings include the diagnosis at birth of congenital heart disease.

His work at the Minneapolis Veterans Administration Hospital is a landmark in diagnosis using the hand. Other researchers study the effects of a brain defect called mongolism. It leaves a distinctive set of markings on the baby's hand, including the Simian Line, which is a complete melding of the head and heart lines so that they run, inextricably mixed, in a straight line across the palm.

Diagnosis of health problems from the hand is extremely difficult, and still far from fully researched so if a problem is suspected from the indications you will learn in this chapter, it is suggested that you visit a physician for a true diagnosis.

FORETELLING THE FUTURE

It would be a mistake to say that an analysis of the hand, even by an experienced analyst, could foretell the future. Hand analysis is not fortune-telling. We can, and do, see and outline present trends which may foreshadow future problems, especially in the area of health. It is our hope that what we or you see will be checked thoroughly by qualified physicians.

My first experience with health was through a Catholic Sister, who joined one of my early classes. She worked at a large local hospital and offered to bring in prints of patients already diagnosed to compare with the hands of people with no physical problems. Within a few days, the class was studying groups of her hospital prints and prints of our own hands and from our files. One of the first diseases that seemed apparent was diabetes, a blood-sugar problem.

Some physical conditions or sensitivities seem to be hereditary, no doubt carried in the DNA of the parents. Other conditions, such as alcoholism, are often found in conjunction with hereditary psychological characteristics; most alcoholics carry the alcohol/drug allergy line upon their hand. This line is known to be hereditarily transmitted from parent to child, although it may, in its active form, skip one or more generations.

ALCOHOL/DRUG ALLERGY LINE

The body, once exposed to the substance to which it has an inborn allergy, seems then to actually *crave* the very substance which will continue to aggravate the allergy. To find this distinctive marking, look at the Health Map (p. 156).

It does not follow that all persons having this line (which was once known as the ''poison line'') on their hands will become alcoholics. The line also indicates that there is a problem with allergies to drugs, even prescription drugs. People with this line may take a pill that would put another to sleep for eight hours, yet it leaves them lively and wide-awake. Others may take a mood elevator which should leave them feeling upbeat, yet the pill's effect is to put them to sleep.

If you have this line upon your hand, or any member of your family has it, it would be wise to alert your physician that you may not react to medicines in the right way, and to try a medication slowly, recording all symptoms, over a period of five days before you begin full treatment with a medication. Before the five days are over, you will know whether you can take that medication or not, and a substitute can be given by the physician. There are some individuals who are allergic to the brand-name drug and not as allergic to the generic form.

Even aspirin, cold medication, allergy pills, or antacids may cause bad reactions if you have this line on your palm. On the left hand only, it is a latent allergy and you may not have much trouble of this sort. On the right hand, if that is your dominant hand, it operates as given above.

Allergies, in general, are easy to spot on the hand, and no test is needed in most cases. If a question arises, have a doctor do a complete allergy profile on you, or the person involved.

THE IMMUNE SYSTEM

Most of us have a strong immune system, which resists the invasion of the body by germs, some viruses, and other microorganisms. We are given some shots as children to make us immune to the prevalent childhood diseases.

What is not known is that not only the tetanus vaccine needs to be "boosted" in adulthood, but several others of our early vaccinations need boosting as well.

On some hands, there is a small fan-shaped formation of tiny lines which appears between the head and heart lines, under the ring and little fingers. (See Health Map.) This "fan" of lines indicates that you may have little or no resistance to "bugs," so that if you are in the presence of a person who has a bacterial or virus-caused disease, you are at its mercy and will inevitably catch it.

Health Map of the
Human Hand #1

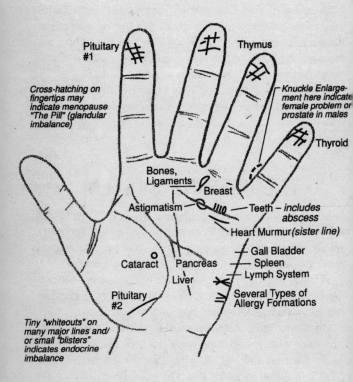

Pituitary #1

Thymus

Cross-hatching on fingertips may indicate menopause "The Pill" (glandular imbalance)

Knuckle Enlargement here indicate female problem or prostate in males

Thyroid

Bones, Ligaments

Breast

Astigmatism

Teeth – *includes abscess*

Heart Murmur *(sister line)*

Gall Bladder

Spleen

Cataract

Pancreas

Lymph System

Liver

Pituitary #2

Several Types of Allergy Formations

Tiny "whiteouts" on many major lines and/or small "blisters" indicates endocrine imbalance

Health Map of the Human Hand #2

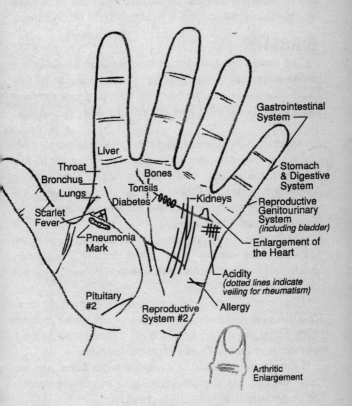

Gastrointestinal System

Liver

Throat
Bronchus
Lungs

Bones
Tonsils
Diabetes

Kidneys

Stomach & Digestive System

Reproductive Genitourinary System *(including bladder)*

Scarlet Fever

Pneumonia Mark

Enlargement of the Heart

Acidity *(dotted lines indicate veiling for rheumatism)*

Pituitary #2

Reproductive System #2

Allergy

Arthritic Enlargement

The most severe cases of this are the children who must live inside a sterile "bubble" without which they are prey to every germ. This severe a case is *extremely* rare.

If you, or someone you love, has this on the hand, it would be wise to limit exposure to persons who have just contracted a cold, flu, or other disease. Only one case in a million would call for the "bubble" form of protection, but if your child has this fan, please be certain that he is taken to a physician just as soon as he shows signs of any illness.

DIABETES

The outward indications of this physical condition are found at the end of the heart line. They appear to be tiny "cuts" or droplets on the line. The cuts look as if the point of a sharp knife were pressed into the line. (See figure, p. 157)

When the hand is ink-printed, they appear as more visible dots clustered within the space of an inch, under the middle finger or, more rarely, under the ring finger. There may be as many as a dozen of these cuts, or as few as three. Apparently, the seriousness of the tendency determines the number of cuts which appear.

If only a few dots appear, all toward the space between the index and middle fingers, then there is a hereditary predisposition to diabetes, although you yourself may not have a problem.

If there are many, covering an inch or more of the heart line, then the likelihood is that you yourself have a problem with blood sugar and should have frequent checks by a physician or with a Diastix from the drugstore.

Diabetes is not caused by eating too much sugar, as some have thought, but is often inherited. It can be activated in older persons or in the very overweight.

Closer to the middle of the area between ring and middle

fingers it may indicate an elevated blood sugar in a younger person.

If the tiny cuts are wide, almost rounded into an island, the indication would be the reverse of diabetes, which is hypoglycemia, or low blood sugar.

It is important to try and get an inked print of the hand to see these "cuts" clearly, although they are visible with the use of a magnifying glass, and a good light. If very faint and hard to see, it is likely that the blood sugar problem is not severe, and may result only in a tiredness in the afternoons.

Comparison of the hand with these tiny "cuts" or dots in a diagnosed case of diabetes with a hand which has no blood sugar problem will be interesting; and once seen, the markings are easily recognizable on any hand on which they appear. If the condition is under medical treatment, the tiny cuts will fade and be less visible.

MIGRAINE AND HEADACHES

The head line may have small, similar markings, almost like tiny cuts made with the point of a knife. These may appear all along the head line, or may be concentrated at one end or the other. Wherever they appear, they indicate a tendency to headaches. If the line is interrupted by a wider "cut," then there may be a problem with migraine headaches. Should you see these deep, wide markings on the head line, look at the little finger and note any horizontal lines which are not deep, but faint or shallow. There is always a possibility that the migraines may be caused by a digestive problem at the beginning, and if the thin horizontal lines appear on the middle and lower sections of the little finger, you will know that this is indeed the cause. If you find both indications, then a "diet diary" should be kept, so that you will know just what you ate before the migraine headache began; and by avoiding these foods you may avoid the migraine.

Stress and tension also create "dots" on the head line, and may appear in the middle section of the head line on many hands, as midlife is usually the portion in which the greatest stress occurs.

Dots all along the head line indicate not only headaches and stress, but might indicate a lack of potassium as well. If this is found to be the case, eating a large number of foods which contain natural potassium (such as bananas, green peppers, paprika, potatoes) may help to alleviate the problem.

EYE PROBLEMS

Problems with vision and eyesight are always indicated by a marking on the heart line under the ring finger or in the space between the ring and little fingers. Usually an island, this is a very small but important indication. The right hand is used, and the right eye will be indicated as above the heart line, with the left eye below the heart line.

If there are no markings or islands in that place, it is likely that the eyes are fairly good. If a problem exists, there will be an islanded formation, indicating in which eye the problem exists. Often, if there is an island only under the heart line and none above, there will be some amount of astigmatism. *(See figures pp. 106, 114)*

Glaucoma is indicated by a tiny, rounded island with a dot in the center of it.

Cataracts, which were once such a problem and now so easy to remove, are indicated by a small round formation between thumb and lifeline, but closer to the lifeline and in the lower part of it. *(See figure, p. 156)*

CIRCULATORY PROBLEMS

Problems with the circulation of the blood are indicated by a "chained" appearance of the heart line. It will not be a large chain, but as if made up of tiny links. Usually, these are not visible in the first half of the heart line, but found in the last third and under the middle or index fingers.

If the heart line begins with a thick three or four-pronged fork, then the blood pressure may be high. If there is a very slight separation of the line, *almost* a fork, but narrow, then the blood pressure may be low. A clean beginning to this line indicates normal blood pressure.

Problems of the heart will be marked as unusual formations in the latter half or near the end of the heart line. Only a specialist should make such a diagnosis, and if you see an odd marking in this position, it may be an old scar or some accidental marking. Everyone should have a thorough physical checkup once a year, and if there are problems, the checkup will locate them.

ARTHRITIS AND RHEUMATISM

These conditions not only affect the joints and knuckles of the body, but are diagnosed by the top knuckles of the fingers themselves.

If there is an enlargement of the uppermost knuckle of the index finger, it indicates rheumatoid arthritis. In this case, *all* of the other knuckles will be normal and not enlarged. Naturally, if the owner has had rheumatoid arthritis for a long time, it is likely that all finger joints will be enlarged and swollen. Rheumatoid arthritis can, however, be diagnosed early in life, before it begins to become a crippling problem.

Osteoarthritis will affect the finger joints by enlarging the knuckle which corresponds to that part of the body which is affected. These are:

Index fingertip	hips and lower back
Middle fingertip	knees
Ring fingertip	legs and feet
Little fingertip	neck and upper back

The enlargement is usually at the sides of the finger joint. It appears early in life, in many cases, and signifies that the owner will develop osteoarthritis sometime in his life. After the disease is active, of course, these spurs and enlargements may appear on all of the finger joints.

Rheumatism has a much less apparent effect on the hand, and will be found on the outside edge, just under the heart line. It appears to have something to do with the acid PH balance of the body. A highly acidic system will have upright vertical lines in this position, and if rheumatism is present, these vertical lines will be crossed by horizontal markings, making a tiny checkerboard-appearing formation.

If a marking of small vertical lines is seen below the heart line with *no* crossing lines, then the system is highly acid, and may be able to resist many types of disease, as the acid is very resistant to yeast infections, some bacterial and virus-induced medical problems. Some years ago, I read a book by a Minnesota physician who advocated the drinking of cider vinegar for these purposes. It seems, however, that many humans have a highly acid system as a natural deterrent, without the vinegar.

Few lines in this area, or none, would indicate an alkaline Ph balance, and the recommendation would be that the owner add a number of acid fruits and vegetables such as tomatoes to the diet to rectify this.

On hands which show the enlarged knuckles of arthritis, it is common to find no acid lines at all.

THE GLANDS

The fingertips are the province of the glands. Diagonal lines on the tips indicate a possible problem in these areas:

index fingertip	pituitary gland
middle fingertip	adrenal glands
ring fingertip	thymus gland
little fingertip	thyroid gland

These lines may be seen around the entire tip of the finger, especially if a problem exists in that gland. Often, in cases of thyroid deficiency, the index fingertip is also seen to have the diagonal lines of pituitary deficiency.

In cases of Hashimoto's thyroiditis, the lines in the little fingertip may be extremely deep and wide.

It would be interesting to compare fingertips of persons with underactive thyroid problems with those of overactive thyroids such as President George Bush and his lovely wife. The signifier of Graves' disease seems to be *horizontal* crossing lines on the sides of the little finger's tip. Very light lines would indicate a less serious condition.

THE DIGESTIVE SYSTEM

Again, the little finger is the indicator of the digestive system, as follows:

tip section	mouth/throat
middle section	stomach/digestive system
bottom section	colon

The most important indication in this area is the marking which indicates that a person has, has had, or may have in the future an ulcer. This indication is a deep line which cuts into the side of the middle section of the little finger. It usually doesn't go all the way across the finger, but only halfway. If deep and red, the indication may be that the ulcer is irritated and active. If light and pale, it may be healed and in the past. If small and reddish, a tendency to ulcer may be present.

If this is visible, then look at the area between the base of the thumb and the lifeline, and see if there are a great many lines radiating from the base of the thumb across to the lifeline, and even beyond. These are known as *worry* lines. Worry lines indicate a person who may be called a "worry wart" as he or she spends a great deal of time fearing possible disasters. If the lines appear only in one area, then that portion of the life is affected. One may be a worrier as a child, then find peace as an adult; or it may be that as an adult he has become a worrier. Sometimes this indication is seen only in one area of the space and the time involved can be estimated from the age of the hand's owner.

LYMPHATIC SYSTEM

This involves the entire outside edge of the palm under the heart line and down to the wrist. If there is an infection in the body, there will be red spots which appear when the lower portion of the palm is pressed downward, or the fingers bent backwards so that the palmar skin is taut. A deep red "blush" in this area can indicate that the person is indulging in too much alcohol as well. Many physicians look for this indication in the hands of suspected alcoholics.

A light reddish blush in this area can indicate an infection of some kind, and may also indicate that the person, if a female, is taking the birth-control pill. In this case, the fingertips will also be cross-hatched with tiny lines.

Small "blisters" which show up on the ink-printed hand are markings of hormonal imbalance, and may be seen on the hands of both men and women.

REPRODUCTIVE SYSTEM

This area spans the lower outside bottom of the palm from the middle of the wrist outward. A reddening in this portion may indicate some problem in the female area. If this is seen, check the inside of the lower knuckle on the little finger. If it is "indented" outward, with a small bulge pushing out toward the ring finger, then there will be problems in the female area of the body if a woman, or possible prostate problems in a man.

A deep red spot exactly in the middle of this area can indicate pregnancy.

Small islands in this area may indicate harmless cysts, or a slight enlargement of ovaries. It is best to check with a gynecologist if redness, islands, or other outstanding markings appear in this area.

LUNGS

On the bulge under the index finger, you will find the area belonging to the lungs. Redness or a reddish spot here may indicate a cold or the flu.

An island on this area may indicate a problem which should be checked by a physician.

In the area immediately between the index finger and the middle finger, very high up on the pad below, are the areas of ear and neck, including tonsils. If an islanded formation appears here, it is possible that the person has swimmer's ear, has had a recent cold or ear infection, or that the tonsils may still be present and the throat is sore. A common sore throat may present a reddish spot in this area, seen most easily when the fingers are pressed gently backward.

KIDNEYS

Most common of the visible kidney problems is the puffy enlargement of the lowest section on the ring finger. This indicates water retention in the body.

It is also seen when the blood pressure is high and indicates that a diuretic may have been prescribed, but forgotten or not taken.

THE FINGERNAILS AND THE SPINE

Most of us think of our fingernails as being all alike. In many cases, this may be true in that they are rounded or square, short or long.

What is not apparent in most cases is that there may be a great deal of difference in the way the nails sit upon the finger. In many cases, they have protuberances, hangnails, depressions, or deep channels running at an angle upon their surface. Some of these indicate dermatological problems, but most of them are indications of the condition of the human spinal column and its normalities or abnormalities.

The fingernails are a reflection of the bony parts of the spine and the discs which form their cushions. Beginning at the thumb and continuing across the hand, the shape and conformation of the nails outlines the condition of the skull and spine, as follows:

Thumbnail	Skull and first two bones of the neck, axis and atlas
Index fingernail	Cervical vertebrae 4, 5, 6, 7 (neck to midway between shoulder blades)

Middle fingernail	Thoracic or dorsal vertebrae (the 12 bones from shoulder blade to waist or mid-back)
Ring fingernail	Lumbar vertebrae 1, 2, 3, 4 (mid-back to pelvic girdle)
Little fingernail	Sacrum and coccyx (pelvis and tailbone)

There are quite a few indications of problems with the spine that may appear on one or more of the fingernails. Statistically, a majority of Americans over 30 have one or more problems with their backs, so it is likely that on your hand, one or more of the nails will be affected.

The best method of checking the nails for these indications is to hold the hand upwards and bend the fingers over toward your face, so that you are looking directly at their tips.

Carefully note the position of each nail, scanning from right to left.

Questions:

Is the nail lying straight on the finger with no sloping to left or right?

Does the nail turn down at the tip, or does it lift up so that you can see the underside?

Does the nail seem to curl at the side, almost like a small hook? If so, does the hook turn down into the finger, or upwards?

Is there a flattish place at the side of the nail before it touches the flesh of the finger?

Is there almost a right-angle bend at one side of the nail? If so, can it be seen from the top of the nail?

These are the most common indications of injury to the spine, and the major cause of backaches.

DEPRESSIONS IN THE NAIL

Most common on the thumbnail, these are small, round depressions that look almost like the point of a nail was driven into the fingernail. This type of depression does not disappear from the nail completely, although it becomes more shallow as the time of the injury becomes distant. It indicates that at some time or other there was an injury to the skull, perhaps a fracture or severe concussion.

Such an indication on any other nail would reflect an injury to one of the bones in that spinal area. They are less common than are skull injuries.

It is possible to have a depression still visible on the hand fifty years or more after the original injury.

TRENCHES OR FLAT PLACES

A deep and narrow flat line which runs from the nail bed to the tip will indicate an old injury to a vertebra. This may indicate that the bone was chipped.

FLANGES

A flange is a flattish area of the nail at one side or the other, indicating that there is pressure on a spinal disc in that area. If the bone is tilted and pressing on the left side, then the flange will be on the left side of the nail. This is often the cause of hangnails; as the flange grows out and butts into the flesh of the fingertip it will tip up slightly and cause a tiny extra projection at the side of the nail.

RIDGES

Deep ridges in the nail may signify back problems, but may also indicate thyroid or other glandular problems. In this case, it is likely that only one nail will be affected. The nail is often ridged, indicating that the neck is permanently

INDICATIONS IN THE NAIL

A depression in thumbnail indicates skull injury. Cross-wise deep "valleys" are often emotional trauma. Skull injury depressions are usually small and isolated, not running all the way across the nail.

A lengthwise "trench" in nail signifies old injury to a vertebra (possibly a chip).

Nail arches should be regular, any irregularity signifies a spinal problem.

Right-angle bend

The flange at one side (disc pressure)

Hook nail

Nail rising out of its bed

NOTE: *Dished nails may indicate anemia or possibly vitamin deficiency. Dished nails are concave instead of convex.*

twisted. In cases of whiplash injury such as that following an automobile accident, the thumbnail may develop permanent malformations, as will the index finger.

Chiropractic, osteopathic or orthopedic remedies may alleviate these problems, but the nail will retain the impression of the previous neck condition.

RIGHT-ANGLE BEND (Tabletop formation)

If the nail has an almost perfect right-angle bend at one or the other side, the indication is that an injury has occurred to the portion of the neck or back indicated by that fingernail. In this case, there may be continuous episodes of pain and backache.

The nail may be tilted to one side, indicating that the person may not stand perfectly straight. In this case, it may appear that one shoulder is higher than the other.

Nail curvature may be visible, even without the sharp bend appearing, and if it is seen, it also indicates that the spine is twisted to left or right, causing pain when sitting, standing, or walking.

This tilt is visible when holding the fingertips toward the face. It can also be seen when the hand is held out palm down. The side of the nail on which the irregular curvature appears will indicate that the same side of the spine is the location of the problem. This rule holds true for all malformations of fingernails.

THE HOOK

When the curvature of the nail curls underneath, or turns in toward the tip, it can form almost a perfect hook, which is the cause of many ingrown fingernails and toenails. In fact, when this nail formation is present, particular care should be taken in cutting finger- and toenails to ensure that this hood does not cause infection through ingrowing and irritation of the tissues at the side of the nail bed.

The hook signifies that there has been a crushing type of injury to a vertebra, or even a break. Such an injury could be caused by falling down a flight of stairs, or even in a fall from a horse or ladder. It has been seen in the case of an individual who dove from too high a board and landed flat on the water.

Usually, the back condition is of some duration, and may be the result of a forgotten incident, although a source of constant pain.

CORRUGATION

A generally corrugated condition of any fingernail indicates that an injury or abnormality to the spine is present, but it is not the same type as would be visible after an accident. It may represent a curvature of the entire spinal column, or any part thereof. Scoliosis can cause tilting and corrugation of the nails. (Slight corrugation may indicate thyroid disease.)

SLANTING NAILS

Any general irregularity of all the nails, such as a general slant of all nails to one side or the other will indicate that there is a lack of balance in the entire spinal column so that the owner walks with the same direction of tilt as seen on the nails. In these cases, the hip and shoulder may both be visibly higher on one side than the other.

DISHING

If the nail is seen to be almost "floating" on the fingertip, with the sides higher than the center, it could indicate that there is a problem with the back in the area corresponding to that nail, or may indicate that anemia may be present, especially if the nails are very pale.

BENT TIPS

If the nail bends down at the tip over the fingertip, there may be spinal problems, but also there may have been a whiplash injury in the past, leaving the nail permanently bent over, even though the injury may have occurred years in the past.

TILTING

Tilting of the nail so that it looks as though it were lifting off the fingertip is an indication of a permanent change in the position of the spine.

It is most commonly seen on the little finger, indicating that the tailbone is tilted out of place. It is also common on the hands of women who have had several children, as the coccyx is displaced during childbirth and may remain slightly out of alignment.

IN GENERAL

The nails should be evenly curved, arched, or flat, depending on the type of nail. All the nails should be of the same type, and evenly shaped to the finger.

If there is an irregularity in one nail, whether it is a depression, tilt, hook, flange, or other misshaping, there will be a corresponding problem in the back.

It is true that some skin problems will cause extreme deformity of the nails, but the indication of neck and back problems are extremely common on most human hands.

COLORATION

A medium pink is the normal color of nails. Any deviation from this color may indicate a problem, such as:

Blue ring at tip of nail	Lack of oxygen in blood
Blue ring at base of nail	Poor circulation (less common—lead poisoning)
Deep red nails	High blood pressure
Pale nails	Low blood pressure or anemia
Yellow nails	May indicate fungus infection or excess beta carotene
Pale mauve nails	Poor circulation, lack of exercise
Bright white nail	Usually on index, may indicate fungus from squeezing citrus fruits
Splitting white nails	Lack of calcium, mineral deficiency

Your fingernails can be important indicators of your general health in both their shaping and color.

Toenails are usually a mirror image of the fingernails, and what is true of the hand will also be true of the foot.

Regular shaping, whether arched or flat, will indicate normal spinal balance, as will regular coloration indicate generally good health.

Any change in a nail should be examined carefully, and a record kept of when the abnormality first appeared. If it persists, a health checkup should be scheduled.

Back pain is one of the most common ''annoyance'' diseases of the human race. It can be detected by misshaping of your nails, and treated promptly. If this is the case, the nail indications will become less noticeable, although they will always retain the old indications in some slight form.

Please refer to Chapter 2 for types of nail shaping and their meanings.

8
YOUR HOROSCOPE ON YOUR HAND

Since the dawn of time, man's interests have turned to two special studies—his relationship with the universe, and his relationship with himself. His equipment for this study was limited, consisting mainly of the lights in the sky we call stars, and the lines in his hand.

Much of the knowledge of the ancient world has been lost or misunderstood. But, since they "builded better than they knew," enough tradition has come down through the centuries for dedicated scholars to reconstruct much of this hidden information.

Do the "stars" (in reality, the planets) have any effect upon man? Modern scientific research has acknowledged that the planets in their orbits not only affect one another, but that our shining satellite, the Moon, rules the tides and weather, as well as the emotions of Earth's inhabitants. The annals of law enforcement and of psychiatry contain much undeniable evidence that the phases of the Moon affect the workings of the mind.

Other studies have shown that men and women born at a particular time of year will be subject to certain physical problems, or live by certain talents and attributes completely different from those born at any other time of the year.

These divisions in time are known as Zodiac signs, which were given names and meanings back in Babylonian times, when each new child's birth was noted with an official horoscope. A horoscope is merely a sort of chart of the sky at the time you were born. It shows where the Sun and Moon were, as well as the other planets that belong to our solar system. The 360 degrees of the circle around which the Earth turns have been divided into twelve sections of 30 degrees each, and then given the name of one of the ancient twelve Zodiac signs. The horoscope maker, called an astrologer, then adds the sign in which the Sun was when you were born, as well as the Moon and the other planets in the sky.

Normally the Sun is considered the most powerful influence in the horoscope. It may also be the most powerful influence on the hand. Its position is the largest, taking in the entire third phalange of the thumb, reaching all the way out to the lifeline. In many hands, this portion of the palm is obviously the largest, and the more highly padded and outstanding this pad, the more importance the Sun's influence should be given in the life, as well as the sign in which the Sun appeared when you were born. A suggested book to use in discovering your own sign and Moon position is listed at the back of this book.

It is often possible to determine in which part of the year a person was born due to the prominence of the portion of the hand which is assigned to that Zodiac group.

If, for instance, you were born in December, and the tip

of the index finger is by far the longest on the entire hand,
then the Sun position in Sagittarius at that time is the strongest influence on your personality. The attributes of Sagittarius that have been gathered and recorded throughou
history would fit you on almost all points.

ASTROLOGY AND THE HAND

The four fingers and their sections, the mounts or fleshy
pads below the fingers, and the general shapes of the hand
are the basis of the relationship of hand analysis and astrology.

The relative sizes of these portions of the hand can be
explored to add more knowledge about the basic personality
This information can be added to what you have already
discovered about yourself, to form an even more complete
picture of your unique personality.

Thumb tip	Intuition	Moon
Thumb middle and base	Outer personality	Sun
Index finger	Ego, self-esteem	Jupiter and Mars
Middle finger	Superego, inner mind, character	Saturn and Uranus
Ring finger	Talents, interpersonal relationships	Venus and Neptune
Little finger	Communication, self-analysis, sex	Mercury and Pluto

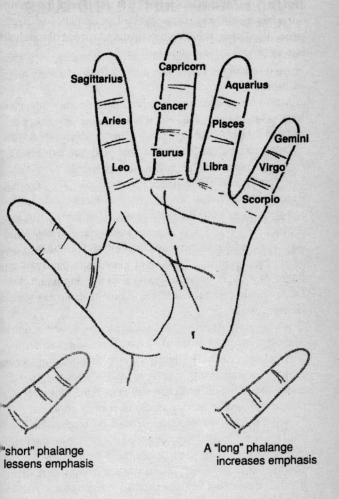

"short" phalange
lessens emphasis

A "long" phalange
increases emphasis

INDEX FINGER—JUPITER AND MARS

On the basis of observation and experience, it has been noted that men and women who have shown great leadership potential, a powerful and influential personality, or a great amount of ambition have inevitably possessed a long finger of Jupiter.

Since the Zodiac groups represented on this finger are Sagittarius, Aries, and Leo, it would seem that this group of strongly motivated Zodiac signs fits the designation well.

Power, ambition, leadership, and goals are exhibited by the development of this finger, and its length.

Psychologically, the finger represents the ego, the outward moral attitudes, the unconscious motivations toward self-betterment or self-improvement. It is the part of personality which lies just beneath the surface of the mind. Insecurity, a false superiority complex, and inferiority complexes can result in a bending or even a shortening of this finger. If a finger is much shorter than the ring finger, both hands should be checked to see if this indication is visible on both hands.

A very short finger might indicate a person who requires some type of psychological "crutch" on which to rely.

If the finger is only slightly shorter than the ring finger, it may indicate only a lack of self-confidence or self-assurance. If the difference in size is extreme, however, the person may suffer from a severe inferiority complex.

A good many people who depend on alcohol have not only the short index finger, but the allergy line on the palm (See Chapter 7.) In such cases, these people are actually allergic to the systemic poisons in alcohol without realizing it. Then the system begins to actually *require* these poisons which have sensitized their systems, and the allergy sufferer becomes an unwitting alcohol dependent—through physical addiction rather than psychological addiction.

The co-rulership of this finger by Mars is the result of an observation that many of the attributes of the finger belong to those ascribed to that planet. Aggression and willpower are considered to be Martian qualities.

If this finger is badly twisted or crooked, this will show that the goals or ambitions of the person may also be twisted or crooked into dishonesty or untrustworthiness.

Habitat of the ego, this finger may be seen bending toward the middle finger, thus indicating that the ego is being ruled by the superego, and that the person's actions may be as a result of deep inner stimulus. This indicates a somewhat possessive personality, and one which is desirous of material security. If *both* upper and middle joints are bent toward the middle finger, it may indicate a passive personality. This should be measured carefully, to see if the finger is actually short, or just bent.

The index finger is called the Jupiter finger, and is a key to the meanings and effects of the remaining fingers.

MIDDLE FINGER—SATURN AND URANUS

This finger is seldom considered overlong, unless the hand is of the Mental or Emotional type and all fingers are found to be approximately equal in length. A short finger of Saturn is rarely seen, and if it is, will indicate one whose personality is shallow. A very short middle finger might indicate a sociopathic personality.

The finger represents the inner personality, the depths of the mind, and the balance between the conscious and unconscious motivations of the personality.

Psychologically, it would relate to Jung's "collective unconscious,'' and represents the intellectual and aesthetic motivations of the owner.

The motivations which are too far below the surface of the mind to become visible are the province of this finger. It acts as a sort of governor, teacher, and your conscience. The basic drives and urges of the ego and superego, prodded by the unconscious mind, are channeled through this finger. Its condition and appearance, therefore, are of extreme importance in the analysis of any hand.

A twist or bend of *this* finger is significant. It may not appear in the print, but can be recognized by the nail facing to the right or the left. It represents a complete departure from the ways in which the individual was raised. For instance, an introverted person might, for one reason or another, become an extrovert—a shy individual might become a leader and public speaker—which would create such a twist or bend of the finger. Stammering country singer Mel Tillis possesses such a finger on both hands. He has overcome his inclination to shyness through singing and acting on the stage.

This is known as the Saturn finger, and includes the attributes of Capricorn, Cancer, and Taurus.

The deepest motivation of Capricorn is to understand and to accept himself, and then to apply his hard-won wisdom to those around him. This finger of Saturn is the most important indication of just where the individual stands in this endeavor. If it is long, strong, and well-rounded, the indication is a good one. If it is marked from bottom to top with the vertical lines of thought and achievement, the personality is a strong and trustworthy guide for family, friends, and all who encounter him.

Capricorn at the tip of the finger represents the influence of self-control over the emotional changeability of Cancer. Taurus, stubborn and material-minded, forms the bottom of the trio, and is eventually dominated and evolved through the process of self-awareness and enlightenment.

RING FINGER—VENUS AND NEPTUNE

This finger represents the creative capacity of the individual, in addition to the type and degree of talent. It is the finger of relationships to others, and the emotions concerned in these relationships.

Psychologically, the Venus finger is the *persona*, the face we wear to show the world—the personality we think we have constructed to show the world. Sometimes we think we have done such a good job of this that no one can see through and tell what kind of person we really are—but don't be fooled—unless we have done an exceptional job indeed, our feet of clay may show through every once in a while, no matter how we try to hide them.

Home of the signs Aquarius, Pisces, and Libra, it is a social barometer, exhibiting by its length and development the capacity of the personality to relate and interact with those people outside the immediate family. If long and well developed, you relate well with others, and your urges are towards being of assistance to your fellow human beings.

If only the middle section is long, then the Piscean traits of idealism come through strongly, and the person may always be a romantic looking for a romance.

A long tip on this finger indicates a good teacher, and if not inclined to being a teacher by vocation, one may teach in other ways, such as in art, personal conversations, or sometimes in just listening to others' problems.

If the bottom phalange is short, then the individual likes small groups and quiet conversations; if long—he's a party animal.

If this finger is much longer than the index finger of Jupiter, then you will find a creative individual who has talent in the arts, music, flower-growing or gardening, writing poetry, or some other creative aspect. Even mechanical design can be most creative and the mark of a true Venus native. If the finger is shorter, noticeably so, then the owner may be shy and noncreative.

Infrequently, the Venus finger is seen to be bent toward the little finger. If it is, it represents one who acts on impulse, following the stimulus of the moment, later rationalizing this in an attempt to fit his or her actions into existing moral or social codes of behavior. Sometimes he cannot explain why he did something, but just felt that it needed doing, so to speak.

If the finger is bent toward the middle finger of Saturn, the personality may be dependent on inner stimulus, unable to act forcefully on his own. It may also indicate a person who is pretending to be something he is not—for instance, a woman who is pursuing a career with all she has, when she would much rather be home raising a family, would have a finger bent toward the middle finger of Saturn.

If just slightly shorter than the index or barely bent to one side or another, it may just indicate a personality that needs strengthening and may benefit from some extra education, as it frequently indicates a person who feels the need of or lack of enough education.

It is a very important finger, especially the tip and base sections that relate to the world around you.

LITTLE FINGER—MERCURY AND PLUTO

This insignificant-appearing finger is perhaps one of the most important on the hand, for in its three sections it encapsules the ability to communicate verbally; the sexual urge and relationships; the ability to analyze self and self-motivations; and the urge to discover the new and interesting.

Psychologically, it stands for the id, the hidden primary unconscious in which are formulated the deepest urges and desires of the human personality. It is the irrational self, for it is not capable of rationalizing without the influence of the balanced hand and the strength of the other fingers.

When the finger is very short, the personality is childlike in its simplicity, and the owner is likely to trust too easily and to take things too literally. This person may have problems with understanding some forms of humor because of this tendency to take things just as they are said. Sarcasm is beyond him.

If the tip section representing Gemini is long, then the urge to communicate is strong. If really overlong, it is known as the "telephone finger" for it is usually found dialing one.

If the finger is long, the person will find some way to communicate, no matter what the cost. This tip belongs to writers and journalists, seekers after information to exchange. The talent will lead in that direction if the tip is long, and if neighboring Venus has a long tip as well, the indication is for the good teacher, melding the communication of Gemini with the urge for social service of Aquarius.

The middle section is the habitat of self-analysis, and this Virgo section is quick in aptitude for figures. On many hands, the Virgo section is quite short, indicating one who does not wish to indulge in too much self-examination, or who does not enjoy mathematics or any branch thereof.

This finger section is also often interrupted by the ulcer mark (see Chapter 7) indicating one whose problems have overwhelmed his ability to cope.

Bottomed by Scorpio, the finger may show a lengthening of that section, or an accentuating of its size or width. If it is well developed, the individual is one who enjoys sex and who seeks it actively. If *very* long, it can be seen as the

Don Juan syndrome, where the person is always looking for the perfect sexual relationship, although it may never be found.

A long bottom section also indicates the natural detective, one who is always trying to discover new areas and fascinated with information. Many police detectives and people involved in this pursuit have this long finger, as does TV lawyer Raymond Burr.

There is a sensual quality to this finger section as well, and these individuals may enjoy silk or satin clothing or pillows and strong colors in art, decoration, and furnishings. They are usually found wearing some form of perfume, male or female, and their taste buds and hearing are usually acute.

THE THUMB—SUN AND MOON

The seat of intuition, the tip of the thumb belongs to the Moon. If it is flat, the intuition or inner knowing is very inactive. Should an individual with such a thumb have a feeling of the intuitive type, he would argue himself out of it, or rationalize it away.

This is also true if the thumb tip is normally padded, but the lower phalange of the Sun is crossed with horizontal lines. In this case, the personality is arguing with itself, trying to use logic where it should be paying attention to those subtle feelings one gets from time to time.

If the tip section is highly padded, then the intuition is strong, and the person may be regarded as a lucky dog or a great gambler, for his decisions seem wild and crazy but always turn out in his favor. *Wall Street Week*'s Ruckeyser has this thumb.

If the thumbnail is turned out away from the palm, almost as if it is trying to look like one of the fingers, then the indication is that the person approves of himself, and is generally satisfied with life. He is a lover of tradition and reveres the past. Actor James Stewart has this thumb.

If the thumbnail is turned completely away from the rest of the fingernails, then the person is a breaker with tradition, willful and innovative. He may have little respect for tradition, but will be making his own way through life. This thumb belongs to people who invent new ways of doing things. Atlantic-flyer Charles Lindbergh and the late actor David Janssen had this thumb, as does CNN's Ted Turner.

It is easiest to see this turning-away aspect when the hand is held flat on a tabletop, or while making a handprint, as the thumb must be rolled sideways to get an impression of the skin pattern.

It is in the bump beneath the thumb that we discover if the person has a violent temper or is a peacemaker. The thumb should rise smoothly out of the outside of the palm with no bump. If there is a visible bump, like a small knob, then the owner has a temper and can lose it easily.

If there is no visible bump, the person is slow to anger and quiet, but if he gets really angry, he can be very dangerous.

If the thumb is set at a sideways angle from the rest of the hand, with the bottom joint forming a 45 degree angle to the wrist, the person is born to use an instrument of some type or to play a game such as baseball, football, pool, tennis, or any sport that requires holding an instrument or ball. People having these thumbs are always sports-minded, even if they do not or no longer participate themselves. Football great's Fran Tarkenton has this thumb, as does tennis star Jimmy Connors.

THE PADDED MOUNTS

Upon the hand there are padded mounts or mounds beneath each finger, and all around the outside of the palm. In antiquity these were given great significance. We find that they have meaning only if they are extremely well padded, or completely absent.

SUN

The most important of these pads is the one at the base of the thumb, representing the Sun. This pad should be developed and resilient to the touch.

If it is full and bouncy to the touch, then you are truly a person of character, interesting and interested.

If it is flat, thin, or hard, the personality may not be as freely developed or there may be some constriction in life which keeps one from assuming the full force of the personality.

A hard, thin, yellow pad indicates astrologically that there is some opposition or bad aspect to the Sun, and a look at the fingers and their sections can reveal what the problem may be.

A thin pad crossed by many lines indicates a weakness in the strength of the individual and a lack of conviction in his actions. Check the index finger for shortness to confirm this judgment.

If this portion of the hand is red and puffy, it does not indicate a problem but merely a strong and forceful mentality, and good health. It may also indicate that the Sun is the most important factor in the horoscope, and you are true to your sign.

KEY WORDS: POWER, STRENGTH, WARMTH, GENEROSITY

The Planetary Pads

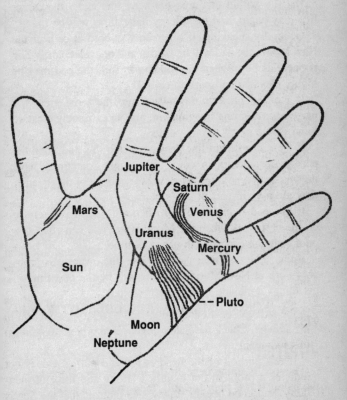

These pads, referred to traditionally as "mounts," are identified by planetary names for ease of identification. They are distinctive when present, more so when absent.

MOON

On the lower outside of the palm, a second large and somewhat elevated pad appears. This is the position of the Moon and its creative, imaginative influence.

Usually within this area the head line ends, the career line may begin, and the allergy indications will be found.

Generally speaking, if a person was born at or near the New Moon, the pad will be flattish and of even color, while if one was born when the Moon was full, the pad may be highly elevated and pink in color.

If the pad projects downward into the wrist area, the person has a strong imagination, and an extremely creative mind is one of his strong points.

If there is a dream line projecting into this pad, then the person may dream in color, and might sometimes have dreams that come true. Whatever the content of the dreams, they are a vivid part of one's being.

If this pad is high and full, then the person is likely to do his best work when the Moon is full and can chart this on a calendar each month ahead of time.

If the fullness is near the head line, the owner was probably born at New Moon, and this will be the best time to get things done and new projects started.

KEY WORDS: IMAGINATION, CREATIVITY, ARTISTIC

JUPITER

This pad is found beneath the index finger, at the top of the palm. If it is high and full, then you are a good leader, full of confidence and optimism. Usually good-natured, you are honest and trustworthy. You will have strong opinions about life and living, politics, and the environment.

If it is just slightly raised, then the person possesses all of the above qualities, but is not as forceful in his opinions.

This individual possesses warmth and sincerity, and is faithful to promises given.

If flat, the person will lack self-confidence and should study his motivations to see what his strengths may be and thus avoid failures which may affect self-confidence.

A small square formed of deep lines on this pad is the mark of the teacher, who can give good advice to those seeking it.

If there are vertical lines on this pad, you may have had to take control of your own life or to head up your own business. A highly padded area here is one indication of a person who was born to follow his own inclinations, and is unhappy working for others. If you are thinking of starting your own business, this is a natural step, and should be successful.

One will probably have reddish hair and a good complexion if this mount is highly padded, as the purely Jupiterian type often has red in the hair.

KEY WORDS: SELF-CONFIDENCE, AMBITION, TRUST, INDEPENDENCE

SATURN

This pad is found under the middle finger. It is not always visible, especially if the Jupiter pad is large and well developed. It may appear to have been "shoved aside," toward the ring finger. In this case, it has the same meanings but there is a strong quality of sensitivity added.

It is on this area that the heart line sometimes ends, and if this is true, the Gift of Mercy is yours.

If this pad is highly padded, the person is sharp of mind, interested in everything and always following a new idea. Research and investigation are their meat and drink and they like nothing better than to find out something they did not already know. Perhaps a teacher by profession, this type will be found teaching his children, family, or friends in some way, if only by example. A favorite gift to receive is a book or puzzle, and personal gifts to others are always either handmade or carefully chosen, and frequently educational in some way.

If this pad is missing entirely, and not pushed to one side or the other, then the person is likely to be easily depressed and have feelings that are easily hurt. They are extremely sincere, but hate to be criticized. This type may be somewhat moody, but it doesn't last.

If pushed into the Jupiter pad, this indication would show a strong appreciation for knowledge and leadership. One might be an inventor, an innovator, or the creator of some new system or process.

If pushed into the Venus pad, this would indicate an artist of some type, whether that art be cooking, gardening, or painting. If it is writing, the creation will be something unique and fascinating. This is possibly the best position for this Saturn pad.

If the pad is right under the finger and highly elevated, the person will have dark hair and possibly dark eyes, may be thin and might have problems with the complexion, eyes, and appetite. This type probably wears glasses.

KEY WORDS: TEACHING, SINCERETY, RESPON-SIBLE, STUDIOUS, HARDWORKING

VENUS

This pad, under the ring finger, is also frequently pushed to one side and combined with either Saturn or Mercury under the little finger. If it is, the signals may be mixed, but they are interesting.

If the pad is combined with the Saturn mound, then the aspect is for a sincere, sympathetic, and warm nature, one attracted to friends among the opposite sex rather than one's own. Thinking is clear and love is not lightly given. This individual is bright, serious, and interesting.

If the pad combines with the mound under the little finger, you are cheerful, happy-go-lucky, with dozens of friends, and love to keep in touch, even with persons you haven't seen in years. You have a tendency to become involved with helping and caring for others, and may take up a career in some aspect of medicine or social work. You love nature and enjoy animals.

Placed directly under the finger, you are charming and attract others without even trying. You are creative and usually wear unusual clothing, with a tendency toward pastels and old-fashioned styles.

This part of the hand exhibits the ability to love and to care for those around you, and if completely missing, the person may be a victim of loneliness and introversion.

KEY WORDS: CHARMING, SYMPATHETIC, TALENTED

MERCURY

This pad, like the fingertip above it, represents ability to express oneself, as well as how fast one thinks. If it is high and pink in color, this is a person who needs to communicate as well as the possessor of a quick-thinking wit. Puzzles, mysteries and games are their meat and they enjoy any sort of intriguing subject.

As a child, such a type may have had trouble separating truth from fiction. Children with this elevated pad also love to read and to hear stories.

There will be an interest in medical matters, and in healing of some type. There may be a strong love of animals and the outdoors as well.

Creativity will be expressed in art or in writing, and the desire to communicate inner thoughts and feeling will be very strong and intense.

If the pad is flattened or missing, this is a close-mouthed person, not forthcoming, who often hates to answer questions, preferring to field a question with one of his own (the answer to which will answer the one asked).

Young people with this mount flat or almost invisible will have problems making friends and communicating with others. They should be encouraged to join groups of some kind with a common interest, such as photography.

As an adult, the person with a flat pad of Mercury should find an absorbing hobby which offers some amount of communication with others interested in the same things. Antique collecting is a natural activity for the Mercury pad person, whether it is highly padded or flat. Collecting books or fountain pens would be a natural.

KEY WORDS: PERCEPTIVE, QUICK-THINKING, INTELLIGENCE, WIT

URANUS

This position in the center of the hand is hardly ever in a raised condition, so it cannot actually be called a pad. If the center of the hand is level, between other raised pads, this is a normal aspect.

If, however, the center of the palm is very deeply hollowed, then the cause may be depression.

Since it is in the center of the hand that all the major skin patterns and lines come together, it is justly represented by Uranus, the astrological planet of "happenings."

KEY WORDS: HAPPENINGS, EVENTS, LIFE CHANGES

NEPTUNE

This is a tiny pad, at the bottom of the palm, just above the wrist and in the center of the palm area. If it is raised, you may have a more "psychic" view of life, perhaps an interest in philosophy or ancient wisdom. You are usually drawn to some type of study of the past or actually of history, and will place a special fondness on artifacts from ancient times. You may find old-fashioned items of interest, collect old recipes or cookbooks and, in general, enjoy relics of yesterday.

If flat, you are pragmatic, skeptical, and hard to convince. A car salesman would have a hard time trying to sell you that car only driven on Sundays by an old lady.

KEY WORDS: INTUITION, REMEMBRANCES, THOUGHTFUL

MARS

This pad is found just at the beginning of the lifeline and in the space between the thumb and index finger. If it is raised upward, then you are unusually courageous. Stuntman Dar Robinson had this pad elevated on both hands.

If the pad is crossed by the intensity line, this is a person who will strive to do things always in his own way, just like the Frank Sinatra song "My Way." They do not take direction from others, but prefer to create their own reality. Strength and fortitude are theirs, and they will fight to the death to defend a principle in which they believe, or a friend who is being attacked or slandered.

When this pad is flat, hollow, or absent, people are cautious and may fear dangerous things. One individual whose hand lacked this pad became a devotee of hang-gliding to overcome a fear of heights. Another, the son of a corporate magnate, wished to become an astronaut rather than enter the family business.

Mars is the planet of strength. It adds a masculine aspect to the hand if elevated, because one will be a straight-line thinker, logical and procedural. A fine attribute for a career in any field which involves a test of skill, knowledge, or has some challenge to meet and conquer.

If missing, the person will avoid all changes in life as well as all challenging activities or situations.

KEY WORDS: STRENGTH, RESILIENCE, RESOURCEFULNESS

As you can easily see, the combination of astrology with hand analysis can add much to your fund of insight about yourself or those around you. You may choose to use the meanings given without the astrological names attached. They offer a valid look inside yourself, no matter the names they carry.

9

YOUR PSYCHIC ABILITIES

It has long been noted that everyone possesses a bit of psychic ability. First confirmed in the Soviet Union when they introduced a plan to bring out these latent abilities in some college students, it has proved possible to train ordinary individuals to use the natural intuition they already have. It is also possible to enhance and strengthen abilities that lie dormant within the human mind, so that they add another dimension to the thought processes.

You, like everyone else in the world, have some amount of ability or talent for ESP (extra sensory perception) and if you can locate it on your hand, you may thus begin to learn how to strengthen it and utilize it to create a richer and fuller life.

Indications on your palm may lead you to a fuller understanding of these abilities as well as the desire to develop them in a natural manner.

195

The Eight Special ESP Abilities

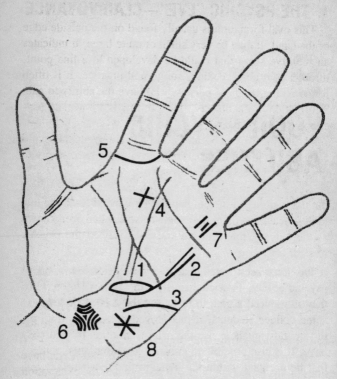

1. The Psychic "Eye"—Clairvoyance
2. Perception—The Psychic Lines
3. Intuition Line—Prediction
4. The Mystic Cross—Inner Knowing
5. Ring of Solomon—Insight
6. Neptune Triradius—Psychic Ability
7. Healing Mark—Touch Therapy Healing
8. Telepathic "Dimple"—Communication Between Minds

1. THE PSYCHIC "EYE"—CLAIRVOYANCE

This oval formation is usually found on the outside edge of the hand. It may be very small or quite large. It indicates an intuitive sense that could be developed to a fine point, through controlled reading, study, and practice. It is often found on the hands of persons who have the ability to gain information from objects. This ability is known as psychometry.

These lines may appear on the hand without the ovoid formation, and in this case you have a special sensitivity to the minds of others.

These lines are more common on the hands of females, but the majority of human hands will show at least one line in this area of the palm. For some reason, it had been known as the "liver" line, but we know it today as the psychic line (or lines).

2. PERCEPTION—THE PSYCHIC LINES

In some cases, these lines run upwards all the way to the pad at the base of the little finger.

The indication is of a special sensitivity, and if you have lines in this formation, you will be drawn to the exploration of your inner self. You may have an interest in philosophy or mysticism.

Your ability to perceive things without knowing how you "know" will usually be strong, and may be developed through usage. At times, you will almost know what others are thinking about if the lines are deep. You may have a natural ability for telepathy, which is the interchange of information between two minds.

This ability may also be developed through practice.

3. INTUITION LINE—PREDICTION

This outcurving line may appear on your hand, and if it does, you will be extremely receptive to the emotions and activities of others. Often, you will know who is calling the moment the telephone rings, or you may dream something that actually happens later on.

If this line appears on your hand you will be good at picking winners or any form of gambling game. You will make the right move at the right time. Others may call you lucky, but it is really a developed sense of what is going on around you, and what may happen in the future as a result of these things.

You may also be precognitive (knowing things before they happen) and often ideas you express will come true later on; and no one will be more surprised than you.

This talent can be developed through exercise and through practice. It is best to have a partner with whom to explore any of the psychic abilities. It is also a good idea to keep a small notebook in which to record any intuitive experiences or events you feel will happen. Your thoughts about these may also be recorded.

This act of recording actually helps to bring out more strongly the ability to predict. Intuition is one of the doorways to the inner mind itself.

4. THE MYSTIC CROSS—INNER KNOWING

This much-misunderstood cross formation appears between the head and heart lines. Rather than being "mystic" in any way, it symbolizes the ability to get heart and head working together. From this standpoint, one will have an almost abnormal ability to know what will happen in the future.

If what you feel you want and what you think you want were to be of equal strength, you would be able to dictate most of the events in your life. Having this ability seems to lend one a deep inner understanding of life and living.

You would be a fine guide and counselor for anyone who has not yet achieved your state of integration of body and mind. Because of this quality, you will have psychic feelings and intuitions, along with an inner "knowing" of what is to come.

Cherish this ability, for it is rare.

5. RING OF SOLOMON—INSIGHT

This is an ancient designation for a deep-cut line which encircles the index finger. It is often found continuing onto the outside of the finger, forming an unbroken circle.

This ring indicates an almost uncanny ability to see the truth about other people, as well as an inner understanding of them, so that nothing they do would come as a surprise.

Compassionate as well as empathetic, these are people who draw others to themselves without even trying, and when they make a friend, that friend is theirs forever.

This unusual ring formation is the mark of a person born to guide or to lead and teach others.

6. NEPTUNE TRIRADIUS—PSYCHIC ABILITY

This formation is found on the pad of Neptune and marks the coming together of three lines of skin patterns. It often has a tiny kernel or triangle where these skin patterns meet. It is an indication that you have psychic abilities of some kind, and you may check the other indications to see which is yours.

If this indication is seen under magnification, it would be wise to explore the subject through reading as many books as possible on ESP ability. You will soon identify which talent is yours and begin to develop it more fully.

7. HEALING MARK—TOUCH THERAPY HEALING

Short, vertical lines at the base of the little finger, on the pad, signify a natural talent or ability for the healing arts. If a career hasn't been chosen in medicine, then one may be well informed on health or some aspect of medical knowledge from reading books and articles dealing with advances in medicine.

Endowed with a natural ability to heal, one may find that just touching someone in pain or distress may bring them peace (touch therapy), or it may actually help in healing. Many great healers have had this mark, although it is found on a large percentage of hands.

8. TELEPATHIC "DIMPLE"— COMMUNICATION BETWEEN MINDS

At the bottom outside edge of the hand, a depression may appear coming in from the edge of the hand. If this depression is visible, especially when you bend your hand forward, it may be the telepathic dimple and you will have the ability to communicate your thoughts to others and sometimes will seem to almost "read the minds" of others to whom you are close in relationship or love. Emotional ties create this kind of bond and two minds in tune will communicate, even if only sporadically.

Exploring this ability can be a great deal of fun. You will definitely need a partner with whom to work.

On almost all hands you will find one or more of these special indications, usually along with a strong head line. The study of ESP today is much different than it was in the

Hand Analysis

Short Capricorn
Poor organization
Prefers not to
take responsible
position

Radial Loop
Fingerprint
"marches to a
different
drummer"!
Career blocks

Long Aquarius tip
indicates person who
should be finding creative
solutions to problems of
others (Social Worker?)

Crossing lines
are blocks. On
this phalange, Leo,
they indicate poor
ego structure

long Gemini
loves to
communicate

Note The
indication
(X) of an
ulcer

Raised
by strong
parents
who shaped
him in
their mold

Note lines
under Venus
finger, very
creative mind.

Logic phalange
did not print.
'By guess and by
golly" system

intuitive
line
formation

alcohol and
breathing
allergies
indicated

This is a male hand of the
Water type. Birthdate Nov. 4.
Note the darkening of the Virgo
phalange. Male water hands indicate very sensitive men.
He has blocking (horizontal) lines on Aries (career) Leo (Ego and
Self-image) Cancer (Emotion) Virgo (probable ulcer)
Water hands have scads of lines all over the palm as this hand
has. Creative, idealistic but blocked in career area

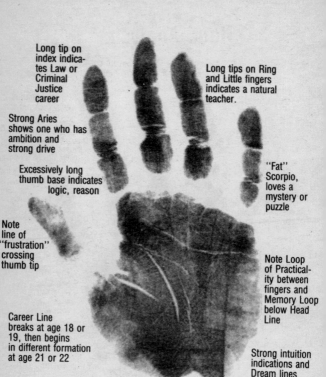

Long tip on index indicates Law or Criminal Justice career

Strong Aries shows one who has ambition and strong drive

Excessively long thumb base indicates logic, reason

Note line of "frustration" crossing thumb tip

Career Line breaks at age 18 or 19, then begins in different formation at age 21 or 22

Long tips on Ring and Little fingers indicates a natural teacher.

"Fat" Scorpio, loves a mystery or puzzle

Note Loop of Practicality between fingers and Memory Loop below Head Line

Strong intuition indications and Dream lines

This is a male hand of the Mental/Action blended type. Birthdate Sept. 12. Owner began a career in electronics and switched to Law School. Is now a practicing Attorney who remembers every facet of any case he takes. Looks forward to appointment to the Supreme Court.

Severe cone on tip
may indicate too organized

Short Aquarius
may lack patience

Fingertip tilted
outward indicates
friendly, open
personality, not an
introspective type

Long Virgo
loves
analysing

Broken "girdle"
overly sensitive
in many areas

Note "fan"
under ring
finger -
many projects

Loop of practicality
between middle and
ring fingers

Has four or more
children

Lifeline chain indicates
severe illness or major
accident before age 18

Dream lines

Small thumbtip
may indicate
will-power needs
boosting

Career Line enters
outside portion
Career probably
journalism, as
forked ending
of Head line would
indicate

Note major lines do not
print clearly. This is
a sign of illness or of
exhaustion

This is a female hand of the Action/Emotional blended type
Birthdate Mar. 12. Artistic, creative and busy, this is a
woman who has successfully raised a number of children and
acquired a career, probably around age 40. Strongly motivated
toward self-education, self-expression. Note fatfingered
"good cook" indication, base of index finger

past, when many of these normal human abilities were considered occult. Today we've learned to accept them as natural and interesting. If you possess one of them on your hand, count it as a lucky "extra" into which you can delve in search of understanding, or allow to grow naturally.

A suggested reading list will be found at the back of this volume for further exploration and study of these psychic talents.

HOW TO MAKE INK PRINTS

Need: Tube of water-soluble speedball ink, any
color
Small rubber roller from any art store
Ceramic tile or piece of flat plastic
One cotton ball
Folded tea towel
8½ × 11 paper
Pencil
(You may wish to use a spiral-bound
sketchbook in which to keep your prints)

Step 1. Do not wash your hands but do remove rings or
bracelets.

Step 2. Place a dab of ink on the tile or plastic and
spread it thin with the small rubber roller.

Step 3. Spread the ink onto the hand, evenly, from
wrist to fingertips.

Step 4. Place hand on the paper, which should be
placed on top of the folded towel, with the
cotton ball approximately under the place where
the center of the hand will fit. This raises the
center of the paper, and the entire palm will
print clearly.

Step 5. With an ordinary pencil held straight up and
down, draw carefully around the entire hand
from one side of the wrist to the other, being
careful to outline each finger.

Step 6. Wash your hands and then write your name and
the date at the bottom right hand side of the
paper. After analysis, place the print in a file
jacket for future reference. Remember that lines
on the hand can change quite a bit in only a few
months, so take prints on a regular basis.

BIBLIOGRAPHY

Bartlett, L. *Psi Trek*. New York, NY: McGraw-Hill, 1981.

Goodman, Jeffrey. *Psychic Archaeology*. New York, NY: Berkley, 1977.

Karaguila, Shafica. *Breakthrough to Creativity*. Santa Monica, CA: DeVorss, 1967.

Landsburg, Alan. *In Search of Strange Phenomena*. New York, NY: Bantam, 1977.

Lyons, B., and Truzzi. *The Blue Sense*. New York, NY: Warner, 1991.

Ostrander, Sheila, and Lynn Schroeder. *Psychic Discoveries Behind the Iron Curtain*. New York, NY: Prentice-Hall, 1969.

Pollack, J. H. *Croiset the Clairvoyant*. New York, NY: Bantam, 1969.

St. Clair, David. *Psychic Healers*. New York, NY: Putnam, 1975.

Stearn, Jess. *A Time for Astrology*. New York, NY: Coward, McCann and Geoghegan, 1971.

Wallace, Irving. *The Book of Predictions*. New York, NY: Morrow, 1981.

Wilcox, Tina. *Mysterious Detectives—Psychics*. New York, NY: Raintree Publications, 1977.